COMPACT *Research*

Inhalants

Drugs

ReferencePoint Press™

San Diego, CA

Other books in the Compact Research series include:

Drugs

Current Issues

Inhalants

by Crystal McCage

Drugs

ReferencePoint
Press™

San Diego, CA

For more information, contact
ReferencePoint Press, Inc.
PO Box 27779
San Diego, CA 92198
www.ReferencePointPress.com

Picture credits:
Maury Aaseng, 31–34, 47–49, 63–66, 81–83
AP/Wide World Photos, 13, 17

Series design:
Tamia Dowlatabadi

LIBRARY OF CONGRESS CATALOGING-IN-PUBLICATION DATA

McCage, Crystal.
   Inhalants / by Crystal McCage.
     p. cm. — (Compact research)
   Includes bibliographical references and index.
   ISBN-13: 978-1-60152-015-9 (hardback)
   ISBN-10: 1-60152-015-8 (hardback)
   1. Solvent abuse—Juvenile literature. I. Title.
   HV5822.S65M33 2008
    613.8—dc22
                                              2007016592

Contents

Foreword

> **"Where is the knowledge we have lost in information?"**

—"The Rock," T.S. Eliot.

As modern civilization continues to evolve, its ability to create, store, distribute, and access information expands exponentially. The explosion of information from all media continues to increase at a phenomenal rate. By 2020 some experts predict the worldwide information base will double every 73 days. While access to diverse sources of information and perspectives is paramount to any democratic society, information alone cannot help people gain knowledge and understanding. Information must be organized and presented clearly and succinctly in order to be understood. The challenge in the digital age becomes not the creation of information, but how best to sort, organize, enhance, and present information.

ReferencePoint Press developed the *Compact Research* series with this challenge of the information age in mind. More than any other subject area today, researching current events can yield vast, diverse, and unqualified information that can be intimidating and overwhelming for even the most advanced and motivated researcher. The *Compact Research* series offers a compact, relevant, intelligent, and conveniently organized collection of information covering a variety of current and controversial topics ranging from illegal immigration to marijuana.

The series focuses on three types of information: objective single-author narratives, opinion-based primary source quotations, and facts and statistics. The clearly written objective narratives provide context and reliable background information. Primary source quotes are carefully selected and cited, exposing the reader to differing points of view. And facts and statistics sections aid the reader in evaluating perspectives. Presenting these key types of information creates a richer, more balanced learning experience.

For better understanding and convenience, the series enhances information by organizing it into narrower topics and adding design features that make it easy for a reader to identify desired content. For example, in *Compact Research: Illegal Immigration*, a chapter covering the economic impact of illegal immigration has an objective narrative explaining the various ways the economy is impacted, a balanced section of numerous primary source quotes on the topic, followed by facts and full-color illustrations to encourage evaluation of contrasting perspectives.

The ancient Roman philosopher Lucius Annaeus Seneca wrote, "It is quality rather than quantity that matters." More than just a collection of content, the *Compact Research* series is simply committed to creating, finding, organizing, and presenting the most relevant and appropriate amount of information on a current topic in a user-friendly style that invites, intrigues, and fosters understanding.

Inhalants at a Glance

Inhalant Abuse

Inhalant abuse is common in poor communities and most common among adolescents. It is common in groups of people who cannot afford more expensive drugs.

Patterns in Inhalant Abuse

Inhalant abuse among adolescents peaked in the 1990s and then began to decline. Since 2004, numbers are once again on the rise. Inhalant abuse used to be more common among young boys, but it is now more common among young girls.

Inhalant History

Anesthetic inhalants have been used for over 100 years to numb pain for medical and dental procedures. Solvent inhalant abuse became a problem during the twentieth century.

Inhalants in Household Products

Dangerous inhalant chemicals can be found in a wide variety of household products: glue, nail polish remover, hair spray, compressed air, aerosols, lighters, whipped cream chargers, gasoline, and countless others. Over 1,000 products have been listed by the U.S. Consumer Product Safety Commission as products that contain abusable inhalants.

Inhalant Legislation

Inhalants are not listed in the federal Controlled Substances Act. However, many states have laws against selling certain inhalant products to minors, and some require retailers to keep a registry of sales. Massachusetts requires products with inhalant chemicals to have additives that make inhaling the product difficult.

Worldwide Inhalant Abuse

According to the National Institute on Drug Abuse, the low prices of inhalants make them a problem in many developing countries in Asia, Africa, and Latin America.

Health Effects

The short-term effects of inhalant abuse include lightheadedness, lack of coordination, agitation, and excitation followed by drowsiness. Some inhalants, such as gasoline and compressed air, affect the rhythms of the heart, which can lead to death. Long-term health effects of inhalants include brain damage, nerve damage, and damage to the heart, liver, lungs, and kidneys.

Sudden Sniffing Death Syndrome

Sudden Sniffing Death Syndrome can result from just one session of inhalant use. The heart's rhythms become irregular, and an adrenaline rush can kill the person. It is important to remain calm around someone who is sniffing an inhalant, though that person could die just from the excitement of hallucinations experienced under the influence of the inhalant.

Treatment

According to the Office of National Drug Control Policy, the number of admissions for treatment of inhalants decreased from 2,311 in 1995 to 1,372 in 2005. Over 40 percent of inhalant admissions in 2005 involved people younger than 20 years of age.

Street Terms

Street terms for using inhalants include "bagging," "huffing," "glading," and "gluey." On the streets, inhalants have been called "poor man's pot."

Overview

"Especially in children, inhalant abuse is an underrecognized form of substance abuse with significant morbidity and mortality."

—Robert M. Julien, *A Primer of Drug Action.*

"Many people mistakenly refer to inhalants as drugs; they are actually poisons. Within seconds of breathing the fumes, the user experiences side effects like slurred speech, dizziness, and nausea. Then it gets worse. Users can pass out and become comatose."

—Libby Ticker, "Fatal Choice."

What Are Inhalants?

Inhalants are a class of diverse substances that are grouped together mainly because they are all inhaled by abusers. All inhalants have important uses as cleaners, paints, adhesives, and so forth, and most inhalants are beneficial when used properly. Anesthetics are a group of inhalants that are used to dull pain during medical procedures. Nitrites are another group of inhalants. They are liquids that are extremely volatile and include amyl nitrite, which expands blood vessels and lowers blood pressure, and nitroglycerin, which is used to treat heart conditions because, like amyl nitrite, it expands blood vessels. Nitroglycerin is also used to make explosives. Amyl nitrites are frequently used illegally as a recreational drug because of their sexual effects. They create a sense of euphoria and relax the muscles in the anus.

Overview

Fuels and solvents are the biggest categories of inhalants and the ones that are not intended to be inhaled for any reason. Fuels include butane, found in lighters, and gasoline. Solvents are chemicals found in glues, paints, correction fluid, and many other household products. The problem with these inhalants is that they are extremely dangerous poisons, meant only to serve humans as cleaners, glues, and fuels. They are toxic, and yet they are everywhere and do produce "highs." These two categories are the biggest concern because they are so frequently abused by children.

Who Abuses Inhalants?

Abuse of fuels and solvents is a twentieth-century phenomenon. Glue sniffing was first reported in the *Denver Post* in 1959. While most experts agree that fuel and solvent sniffing did occur before 1959, that article gained national and worldwide attention for the problem and actually seems to have had the opposite of the desired effect by spreading knowledge about solvent sniffing to people who had never before heard of it.

Today, abuse of fuels and solvents is a serious problem in the United States and other countries around the world. In the United States children and adults from lower socioeconomic classes are the most common abusers of inhalants, with children making up the largest number of inhalant abusers. According to Sophia F. Dziegielewski, author of *Understanding Substance Addictions*:

> **All inhalants have important uses as cleaners, paints, adhesives, and so forth.**

The highest rates [of inhalant use] occur among adolescents in the eighth grade, with approximately 20 percent having tried inhalants at least once. Another significant group of users were adolescent Native Americans who lived on reservations, with rates between 25 and 30 percent, including females. [Researchers] examined Native American youth who do not live on reservations to determine possible ethnic influence and concluded that peer influence and socioeconomic stressors were more indicative of potential inhalant abuse. . . . Hispanic adolescents are just as likely as Caucasians to abuse inhalants. . . . Use is related to socioeconomic levels and is more common in isolated rural settings where other substances may be less accessible.[1]

What Are the Short-Term Dangers of Inhalants?

The risks associated with inhalant abuse depend on the type of inhalant. Risks associated with fuels and solvents are much more significant than with other types of inhalants. However, even nitrites, which are frequently prescribed by doctors to regulate problems with the heart and blood pressure can have side effects that include dizziness, weakness, and headaches. Nitrous oxide, an anesthetic used by dentists and doctors performing minor medical procedures, is very dangerous when it is used outside of medical situations. People who illegally use nitrous oxide run high risks of accidents due to impaired judgment and loss of motor control. They may even lose consciousness.

> **The risks associated with inhalant abuse depend on the type of inhalant.**

Short-term risks of abusing fuels and solvents are high. Users experience excitement, which is followed by drowsiness, lightheadedness, and agitation. Loss of consciousness is also possible. The biggest short-term risk, however, is called "Sudden Sniffing Death Syndrome" or SSDS. Sniffing certain chemicals found in solvents and fuels results in irregular heart rhythms. The chemicals also cause cells in the heart to become more sensitive to adrenaline. This is a dangerous combination that all too frequently results in death. Experts point out that Sudden Sniffing Death Syndrome can happen any time a person abuses inhalants, even the very first time.

What Are the Long-Term Dangers of Inhalants?

Prolonged exposure to inhalants can result in serious and, frequently, irreversible damage to the body. Chronic inhalant abusers suffer damage to the heart, lungs, liver, and kidneys. Moreover, like the short-term risks associated with inhalant abuse, the long-term risks vary according to the type of inhalant. Long-term exposure to nitrous oxide results in nerve damage and neurological problems. Long-term exposure to sol-

This can of air freshener was found with the body of a 10-year-old boy who had been inhaling the chemicals to get high at an after-school program in Pittsburgh. Coroner Cyril Wecht, pictured, addresses rising inhalant use at a press conference shortly after the boy's cause of death was determined.

vents damages the central nervous system, including the brain. Researchers have found, for example, that exposure to toluene, a chemical found in glue, results in damage to the cerebellum, which is responsible for coordination and motor function, as well as procedural memory. New research has also shown that the cerebellum plays some role in attention and the processing of language. One research study also found that people who had chronically abused inhalants scored well below the average population when it came to cognitive functioning.

What Are the Effects of Inhalant Abuse on Society?

Inhalant abuse, especially by children and the poor, is a big concern all over the world. When interviewed, these abusers mentioned the need to "escape" problems like homelessness, hunger, and a general feeling of hopelessness. Journalists such as Emily Wax of the *Washington Post* work to bring attention to this issue. In a 2007 article on young homeless boys in Sudan, Wax highlights the terrible living conditions for a group of boys called "glue boys." These boys are homeless and starving and use glue to escape their problems.

> **Inhalant abuse, especially by children and the poor, is a big concern all over the world.**

Crime is also a concern when it comes to inhalant abuse. Research indicates that inhalant abuse often leads to aggressiveness and crime. Certainly, the effects of inhalant abuse are complicated, but awareness, thanks to strong educational campaigns and more media attention, is growing. And as awareness grows, state and local legislators are getting involved.

What Laws Exist to Prevent Inhalant Abuse?

Currently no federal laws regulate the sale or the abuse of most inhalant chemicals. The chemicals found in solvents are not regulated by the Controlled Substances Act, even though they are very dangerous. The reason is that these chemicals are found in products that people need to use every day in their homes and on their jobs. It is difficult for the government to regulate products that people need to use so frequently for perfectly appropriate reasons. About 40 states have passed laws limiting the sale of certain chemicals to minors and outlawing inhaling to become intoxicated. One state, Massachusetts, has passed a law that those involved in inhalant abuse education, such as the National Inhalant Prevention Coalition, see this as one of the best ways to stop inhalant abuse. Massachusetts has passed legislation that requires companies that make products frequently abused as inhalants to add chemical deterrents. For example, it is possible for manufacturers to add stinging deterrents to their products to make inhaling painful and almost impossible. In fall 2006, Falcon, the maker of "Dust-Off," a can of compressed air used most often to clean computers, announced a new version of its "Dust-Off" product that includes a deterrent to inhalant abuse. "Dust-Off" has received a lot of media attention in the last few years because of the reports of deaths associated with inhaling this product. According to Falcon's Web site:

> **It is difficult for the government to regulate products that people need to use so frequently for perfectly appropriate reasons.**

> While entirely safe when used as directed, compressed-gas dusters are one of many aerosol products too often abused by young adults searching for a cheap and sometimes deadly high. In an attempt to discourage this dangerous practice of inhalant abuse, Falcon developed a new formulation for its dusters, incorporating an additive that makes the contents of the can extremely unpalatable to those who attempt to abuse them. The additive was developed to have no adverse effects with normal, recommended use.[2]

While legislation requiring more companies to follow Falcon's lead may reduce inhalant abuse, the greatest focus of most national organizations has been on education about the dangers of inhalant abuse.

What Educational Programs Exist to Prevent Inhalant Abuse?

During the 1990s inhalant abuse among adolescents reached all-time highs. As such, media attention for inhalant abuse grew, and national organizations like the National Inhalant Prevention Coalition and the Partnership for a Drug-Free America began working to better educate the public about the problem. Both national organizations and state departments of education began to focus on the dangers of inhalant abuse. Public schools across the United States now begin basic inhalant education as early as kindergarten. In kindergarten classes students are taught basic information about identifying dangerous substances. Since inhalant abuse can begin as early as age five or six, this seems to be the right time to teach children which substances that are commonly found in the home can cause them harm. For older students, educational campaigns emphasize the risks associated with inhalant abuse. Students are taught about Sudden Sniffing Death Syndrome and the short- and long-term effects of these chemicals.

To put a face to the stories, parents who have lost children due to inhalant abuse now work with national organizations and local school districts to teach children about the dangers of inhalants. One such example is Toy Johnson Slayton of Georgia. She lost her son Bryant, who was 16 years old when he died from inhalant abuse. He went to the store to purchase a magazine but huffed butane before he drove home. His car hit a tree, but according the coroner, he was dead before the car accident. Slayton and parents just like her across the country have now "made it their mission to talk to kids, parents, educators and law enforcement about the dangers of inhalants."[3]

> **Public schools across the United States now begin basic inhalant education as early as kindergarten.**

Ultimately, most experts agree that parents must also be educated to prevent inhalant abuse, so media campaigns have been launched for this purpose. State and local governments are also working harder to educate parents. One example of this is the National Inhalant Prevention Coalition's National Inhalants Prevention Week, held every year in March. During this week the media and local organizations focus on bringing inhalant abuse and its dangers to the public's attention. According to Harvey Weiss, founder of the National Inhalant Prevention Coalition:

This can contains a commercial spray duster often used for cleaning key-boards. Traces of the chemical were found in the bodies of four high school girls who were killed in a car accident in Philadelphia.

Surveys indicate that parents are still behind when it comes to awareness of inhalant abuse in their homes. A lot of times I hear parents whose child has died from inhalants say, "I didn't think my child would abuse inhalants so I never talked to them about it." The problem is—and there has been significant research in this area—that parents are very aware that inhalants can be very dangerous, if not fatal, but many do not believe that their child would use an inhalant. If they don't think their child would do it, they tend not to talk about it. [A study] was done by the University of Kentucky that found 9 out of 10 parents do not believe that their child would use an inhalant.[4]

What Are the Treatment Options?

Inhalant abuse treatment is important because the risks of abuse are so great. Generally, inhalant abuse is treated like other drug addictions, though there is concern because the number of relapses is high. One problem is that inhalant chemicals are stored in the fatty tissues and therefore can remain in the body longer than many drugs do. Therefore, detoxification takes longer, and some drug treatment centers are not aware of this. Inhalant abusers with resulting brain damage also present a problem in treatment, as their intellectual functioning may not ever be normal. According to inhalant abuse experts:

> Abusers with resulting brain damage also present a problem in treatment, as their intellectual functioning may not ever be normal.

The "typical" 28 day or current treatment stay is probably too short a time to realistically expect change. One of the reasons for this is the prolonged time that inhalants persist in the body. Treatment time is uncertain and typically requires many months. Intensive aftercare and follow up are essential to rebuild life skills and re-integrate the client with school, family and community.[5]

Inhalant-abuse treatment centers are especially important, because each time a person sniffs an inhalant he or she could die. The sooner abusers get help, the greater are their chances of staying alive.

How Big Is the Problem of Inhalant Abuse?

According to a 2005 National Survey on Drug Use and Health (NSDUH), "22.7 million Americans aged 12 or older reported using inhalants at least once during their lifetimes, representing 9.4 percent of the population aged 12 or older."[6] Additionally, the people most likely to abuse these chemicals are children. This presents a big problem for society. Surveys such as the Monitoring the Future study indicate that while inhalant abuse declined at the turn of the twenty-first century, it is once again on the rise among children. Abuse is also high among the lowest socioeconomic classes, who cannot afford other drugs but may wish to "escape" the difficulties of their lives. And this is not just a problem for the United States. Countries all over the world struggle with inhalant abuse, especially in areas of poverty. While experts disagree as to what the solutions to this problem are, it is clear that inhalant abuse is a serious issue for many countries.

What Are Inhalants?

❝ Kids who abuse inhalants often sniff them, either by snorting fumes from containers or spraying aerosols directly into their noses or mouths. Kids also may huff these products, soaking rags in inhalants and pressing the rags to their mouths.❞

—Mayo Foundation for Medical Education and Research, "Inhalant Abuse: Help Your Child Understand the Risks."

❝ The easy accessibility, low cost, legal status, and ease of transport and concealment make inhalants one of the first substances abused by children.❞

—U.S. Drug Enforcement Administration, "Drugs of Abuse."

Inhalants are a diverse group of substances, grouped together not by their effects on the body or the brain but by their method of ingestion. These psychoactive substances (substances that affect the central nervous system and alter brain functions) are found in over 1,000 household products, such as canned air, glue, air fresheners, and correction fluid. Some inhalants were developed originally as anesthetics, and some were never meant to be inhaled by humans at all, developed as cleaners or adhesives to be used in the workplace and at home.

Because inhalants can be found throughout the average home, children are particularly susceptible to these chemicals and their dangers. Moreover, inhalants provide users with a cheap high. Users may feel euphoric, delirious, or effects similar to a light state of anesthesia. Most users, especially children, are completely unaware of the dangers of inhalants, as inhalant abuse can go largely unrecognized by parents and is often not an issue parents think about. Parents are often much more aware of drugs like marijuana and alcohol and do not consider talking to their children about things like paint and glue. However, because of the easy availability of inhalants, children are susceptible to abusing them.

What Are the Different Types of Inhalants?

Because so many substances can be abused as inhalants, it is perhaps easiest to group them into categories in order to list and describe them. Inhalants fall into four categories: solvents, fuels, nitrites, and anesthetics.

Solvents

Often called "volatile solvents" because they evaporate quickly, solvents can be found in glues, spray paints, hair spray, nail polish, and correction fluid, to name a few. These products sometimes even contain a variety of solvents. One of the most common solvents is toluene, the main solvent in many glues, and it can also be found in paint, varnish, and nail polish. Trichloroethylene is a solvent used as a degreaser and can be found in spot-removing products and correction fluid.

Fuels

Many fuels are also abused as inhalants, including butane, which is found in lighters, and gasoline. Propane, which is now available in pressurized aerosol cans, is also a fuel commonly abused as an inhalant.

Nitrites

Nitrites are yellow, volatile, and flammable liquid chemicals that can smell bad like dirty gym socks or smell sweet like fruit. Nitrites include amyl nitrite, butyl nitrite, and nitroglycerin. Amyl nitrite is available by prescription and has been used by physicians to treat some heart

> " Psychoactive substances (substances that affect the central nervous system and alter brain functions) are found in over 1,000 household products, such as canned air, glue, air fresheners, and correction fluid. "

conditions. Other nitrites have been prohibited by the Consumer Product Safety Commission and so are not readily available like solvents and fuels are. However, these chemicals are still sold illegally, usually packaged in small, brown bottles and labeled as "room deodorizer" or "liquid aroma." Nitrites relax the smooth muscles that control the diameter of blood vessels and the iris of the eye as well as keep the anus closed and keep the bladder from dribbling urine. Because of their impact on smooth muscles, amyl nitrite has been popular for its sexual effects. It has been popular among homosexuals, for example, and it is estimated that nearly 250 million recreational doses are consumed every year in the United States.

> The increase [in this dangerous use of inhalants] is actually linked to efforts to stop it.

Anesthetics

Anesthetics can also be inhaled. Nitrous oxide or "laughing gas" can be found in everyday products such as helium balloons or in cans of whipped cream.

What Is the History of Inhalants?

Unlike nitrous oxide, which was used recreationally throughout the late-eighteenth century and all of the nineteenth century, solvents and fuels were not used recreationally to such an extent. In fact, before 1959 very few reports were recorded of people deliberately sniffing the fumes from solvents or fuels. However, by the end of the 1960s inhalant abuse had become a serious problem, and some laws were passed against it. The increase in abuse is actually linked to efforts to stop it. A 1959 article in the *Denver Post* reported the arrests of several children in Tuscon, Arizona, and Pueblo, Colorado, for sniffing glue. The article also reported detailed instructions on how the glue was sniffed and what the effects were. According to William A. McKim, author of *Drugs and Behavior*, "Prior to this account, Denver police knew of no cases of deliberate glue sniffing, but by June 1960, they had investigated some 50 cases of glue sniffing."[7] This pattern repeated itself in cities all over the United States, such as New York and Salt Lake City, and by 1968 public concern was high enough to warrant anti-glue-sniffing laws in 13 states. Sniffing of solvents and fuels has continued over the last half-century.

How Are Inhalants Used Today?

According to the U.S. Drug Enforcement Administration, the largest group of inhalant abusers are children between the ages of 10 and 12. Because parents often know little about inhalants, such use often goes undetected. While efforts to educate parents about the dangers of inhalants have occurred in recent decades, parents are much less likely to talk about the dangers of inhalants than of alcohol, tobacco, and other drugs. The 2002 National Survey on Drug Use and Health reported that over 1 million additional people used inhalants during that year. And by 2003 almost 23 million people over the age of 12 reported abusing an inhalant at least once during their lifetimes.

What Are the Effects of Inhalants?

Even though there are a wide variety of inhalants, most of them have similar effects on the body. Essentially, they change the way the brain functions by cutting the supply of oxygen, which is then replaced by the chemical being inhaled. Users report that most often the effects of inhalants are similar to those of drinking alcohol. Unlike alcohol, however, inhalants are sometimes reported to cause visual and auditory hallucinations. Chronic side effects of sniffing inhalants include nosebleeds, nasal ulcers, and nose, mouth, and eye irritation. Long-term effects from heavy inhalant use include mental impairment and the loss of hearing, smell, and memory. According to a 2002 study of 55 inhalant abusers,

> **Inhalants also have serious negative effects on the nervous system, and while many of the long-term effects will disappear once the inhalant abuse stops, growing research indicates that some of the effects on the nervous system and other organs may be permanent.**

long-term inhalant abusers scored well "below general population averages on tests of cognitive functioning." In fact, inhalant abusers "scored even below cocaine abusers on tests involving working memory, planning, and problem solving."[8]

Inhalants also have serious negative effects on the nervous system, and while many of the long-term effects will disappear once the inhalant abuse stops, growing research indicates that some of the effects on the nervous system and other organs may be permanent. Chronic users may become delusional and may show symptoms of schizophrenia, a disorder characterized by loss of reality and by significant social dysfunction.

> " Often children and teens are unaware of just how dangerous these drugs are and that you can die from just one dose. "

Long-term users also sometimes develop tremors. Additionally, damage to the retina and optic nerve has been reported, as has damage to the cortex and cerebellum. Those who abuse nitrous oxide on a long-term basis may have nerve damage, causing weakness, loss of dexterity, and loss of balance.

Inhalant abuse has also been connected with kidney damage and liver damage. Research studies on people who suffer from long-term exposure to inhalants, such as painters and dry cleaners, indicate that men experience a decrease in fertility. And recent research from the late 1990s describes problems in the fetuses of pregnant women who abuse inhalants. Symptoms are similar to those of fetal alcohol syndrome and include low birth weight, facial malformation, and finger and toe malformations.

Why Do People Abuse Inhalants?

Despite the dangers, inhalant abuse remains a problem in the United States and other countries, especially among young people. According to the National Inhalant Prevention Coalition, there are 4 main types of inhalant abusers. The "transient social user" has a short history of use and is likely to use with friends. This type of user is usually 10 to 16 years old. The "chronic social user" has a longer history of use, usually 5 years or more. This type of user uses daily with friends and may have experienced minor legal trouble. This user usually has poor social skills, limited education, and is 20 to 30 years old. The "transient isolate user" is different in that he or she usually abuses inhalants alone. This type of user has a short history of use, and like the "transient social user" is usually 10 to 16 years old. The final type of user identified by the National Inhalant Prevention Coalition is the "chronic isolate user." This type of user has a long history, usually five or more years, of daily, solo inhalant abuse. This person would have poor social skills, limited education, some brain damage, and may have experienced trouble with the law. This type of user, like the "chronic social user" is usually 20 to 30 years of age.

Young children who make up the "transient social user" and "transient isolate user" groups are perhaps the biggest concern for society. People want to know what can be done to stop the abuse at an early age. Many times, children experience peer pressure to experiment with inhalants. Often children and teens are unaware of just how dangerous these drugs are and that you can die from just one dose. According to Jennifer James, author of *All About Inhalants: A Special Report for Young People*, some people "might think that since the products that inhalants come in are legal, sniffing must not be a big deal."[9]

What Are Inhalants?

66Inhalant use starts early; long-term abusers are among the most difficult drug abuse patients to treat. It is critical research efforts intensify, so effective preventions, interventions, and treatments are developed.99

—Nora Volkow, in Rob Chepesiuk, "Resurgence of Teen Inhalant Abuse," *Environmental Health Perspectives*, December 2005.

Volkow became the director of the National Institute on Drug Abuse (NIDA) in 2003. She has a long record of research on drug abuse and has published over 300 articles in peer-reviewed journals.

66A case of suicide due to plastic bag suffocation and ether inhalation is reported. The remarkable point is that the victim followed instructions from the Internet and a respected international financial magazine.99

—Sotiris Athanaselis, Maria Stefanidou, Nikos Karakoukis, and Antonis Koutselinis, "Asphyxial Death by Ether Inhalation and Plastic-Bag Suffocation Instructed by the Press and the Internet," *Journal of Medical Internet Research*, 2002.

Athanaselis, Stefanidou, Karakoukis, and Koutselinis are physicians in the Department of Forensic Medicine and Toxicology in the Medical School at the University of Athens, Greece.

* Editor's Note: While the definition of a primary source can be narrowly or broadly defined, for the purposes of Compact Research, a primary source consists of: 1) results of original research presented by an organization or researcher; 2) eyewitness accounts of events, personal experience, or work experience; 3) first-person editorials offering pundits' opinions; 4) government officials presenting political plans and/or policies; 5) representatives of organizations presenting testimony or policy.

“Adolescents really know little about drugs compared to what they think they know. They are often shocked when they learn how much damage drugs really do.”

—Michael Rios, in Constantina Boudouvas, "Excessive Behavior May Target Spirituality," *Perspective Magazine*, 2004. www.menningerclinic.com.

Michael Rios is a chemical dependency counselor from the Adolescent Disorders Program at the Menninger Clinic, a psychiatric treatment center in Houston, Texas.

“More confident children are more likely to be sociable, have more money and thus have more opportunity to experiment with drugs.”

—Tony Palmer, "Chroming and Harm Minimization," paper presented at the Inhalant Use and Disorder Conference, Australian Institute of Criminology, July 2003. www.aic.gov.au.

Palmer is a trainer/consultant for the Youth Substance Abuse Service in Australia, an organization providing treatment and support to young people aged 12 to 21 years, who are experiencing problems related to their use of alcohol and other drugs.

“In third grade we were getting high on pens and ditto machine fluids.”

—Tiassa, "Drug Free," Science Forums, September 2001. www.sciforums.com.

"Tiassa" is an anonymous contributor to a drug-related discussion group found on the Internet.

66The NIDA annual high school survey reports a lifetime incidence of inhalant abuse of 15% to 20%, but underestimates the true prevalence because school dropouts, who have a higher incidence of substance abuse, are not included.99

—Milton Tenenbein, "Inhalant Abuse: A Policy Statement of the AAP," *Pediatrics*, 1996.

Tenenbein is a physician at Children's Hospital in Winnipeg, Manitoba. He is a member of the Commission on Substance Abuse and the Committee on Native American Child Health.

66Despite national efforts to warn of the dangers, information about the terrible toll inhalant abuse is inflicting does not seem to be reaching the nation's parents, much less their children.99

—Gerry Everding, "Inhalant Abuse on the Rise," *Record*, Washington University in St. Louis, 1999.
http://record.wustl.edu.

Everding was a journalist for the *Record,* the newspaper of Washington University in St. Louis, Missouri.

66A continuing problem in the prevention and treatment of inhalant problems is the scarcity of research findings to guide these efforts.99

—Texas Commission on Alcohol and Drug Abuse, "Understanding Inhalant Users," 1997.

The Texas Commission on Alcohol and Drug Abuse is a state agency that provides educational materials on substance abuse, develops prevention, intervention, and treatment programs, and researches substance abuse in the state of Texas.

"I encourage parents to make homes safer by keeping toxic substances sealed and out of reach ... of children."

—George W. Bush, "National Poison Prevention Week," 2007. www.whitehouse.gov.

George W. Bush is the forty-third president of the United States.

"Stigma might play a role in the potential underreporting of inhalant related indicators (e.g. deaths, emergency room visits, and treatment admissions) as well as in the lack of research on inhalant abuse."

—Robert L. Balster, in National Institute on Drug Abuse, "Inhalant Abuse Among Children and Adolescents: Consultation on Building an International Research Agenda," November 2005.

Balster is a biopsychology professor at Virginia Commonwealth University and director of the Institute for Drug and Alcohol Studies. An active researcher, Balster works on the application of scientific research to the development of drug abuse policy.

"People, their parents, won't know 'cause they got it right underneath their noses. It's not like they are bringing something in the house because it's already in the house."

—Anonymous, quoted in Massachusetts Department of Education, "What We Know About Inhalant Abuse in Massachusetts," 2001. www.mass.gov.

A young student interviewed during a 2001 Massachusetts Youth Risk Behavior Survey sponsored by the Massachusetts Department of Education.

"Sniffing glue is something that we experienced in Forest Hills which is very bad and we found that out quickly."

—Johnny Ramone, quoted in Letta Tayler, "Sounding Off in Suburbia," *Long Island: Our Story*, 2007. www.newsday.com.

Ramone of the punk-rock band The Ramones commenting on the autobiographical nature of their song "Now I Wanna Sniff Some Glue."

Facts and Illustrations

What Are Inhalants?

- Some of the "street names" for butyl nitrite are "Aroma of Men," "Crypt Tonight," "Hardware," "**Lightning Bolt**, "Poppers," and "Toilet Water."

- While Joseph Priestly is credited with discovering nitrous oxide in 1772, Sir Humphry Davy is recognized with discovering its euphoric properties, naming it **"laughing gas"** in the 1880s.

- Nitric oxide, a toxic industrial gas, is occasionally mistaken for nitrous oxide. Inhaling **nitric oxide** can permanently damage the lungs or kill.

- **Inhalation anesthesia** has been regarded as the United States' most important contribution to medicine.

- A common use of inhalants today is in **dentistry**.

- The first aerosol can was patented on **November 23, 1927**, by engineer Erik Rotheim. The spray can he invented was the first that contained a propellant. This was the first of a long line of products that would be very useful as well as damaging.

- **Halon** is a chemical found in some fire extinguishers. It has become a popular "huffing" source because it can cause hallucinations. It can also kill due to its effects on the heart.

Only 5 Percent of Parents Believe Their Child Has Ever Abused Inhalants

According to a 2005 Partnership Attitude Tracking Study conducted by the Partnership for a Drug-Free America, 5 percent of parents believe their child has abused inhalants. According to the study, parents often aren't aware of or are in denial about the prevalence of inhalant abuse among teens. Teens are four times more likely to report abuse than parents believe they will.

Do you think your child has ever experimented with inhalants?

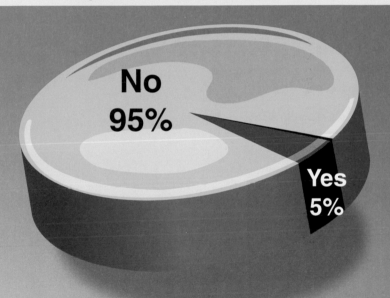

No 95%

Yes 5%

Source: The 2005 Partnership Attitude Tracking Study (PATS), the Partnership for a Drug-Free America. www.drugfree.org

- According to the Keswick Addiction Recovery Center in New Jersey, **25 percent** of adolescents using inhalants for the first time have never indulged in anything else—not even alcohol or cigarettes.

- Inhalation of **amyl nitrite** increases the risk of cancer by increasing the body's production of carcinogens and suppressing the immune system.

Percent of Students Reporting Inhalant Use in 2006

According to the Office of National Drug Control Policy, 29 percent of eighth graders, 40 percent of tenth graders, and over half of twelfth graders reported lifetime use of inhalants in 2006. Numbers for use in the past year and the past month were also high.

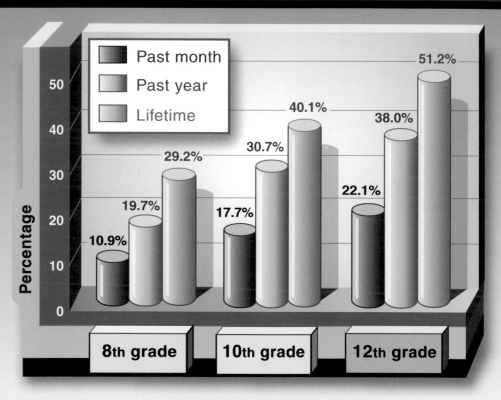

Source: Office of National Drug Control Policy, "Drug Facts: Inhalants," 2007. www.whitehousedrugpolicy.gov.

Percent of College Students/Young Adults Reporting Inhalant Use in 2004/2005

According to the Centers for Disease Control and Prevention, the number of college students in 2004 and 2005 who reported lifetime inhalant use was lower than the number of young adults who, in the same year, reported lifetime inhalant use.

	Young Adults		College Students	
	2004	2005	2004	2005
Past month	0.3%	0.2%	0.4%	0.3%
Past year	1.7%	1.3%	2.7%	1.8%
Lifetime	11.6%	10.3%	8.5%	7.1%

Source: Office of National Drug Control Policy, "Drug Facts: Inhalants," 2007. www.whitehousedrugpolicy.gov.

- More than **one person** dies every week in the UK from the effects of solvent abuse, between 70 and 100 each year.

- Inhalants are considered **highly addictive**, in part, because the "high" inhalant abusers experience is over so quickly, enticing the abuser to use more and more frequently.

- According to a 2001 survey of drug use among Australian youth, over **60 percent** of those who reported using inhalants said they obtained the inhalants from friends.

Inhalant Use Rises Among Adolescents

After a sharp decline in inhalant use, which some attribute to the extensive educational and media campaigns of the late 1990s, inhalant use among eighth, tenth, and twelfth graders in the United States is once again increasing.

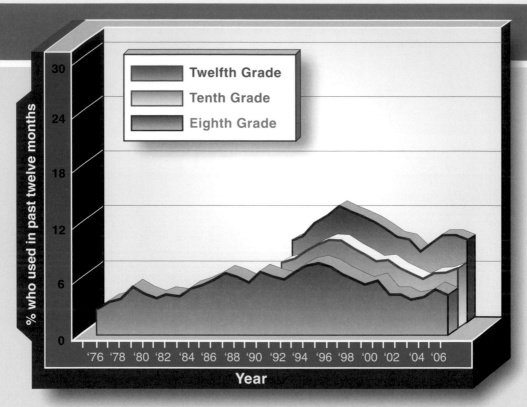

Source: Monitoring the Future Study, University of Michigan, 2006.

What Are the Risks of Inhalant Abuse?

"After the first 3–4 hits I did not feel much, so I kept spraying as I quickly inhaled through my mouth and out through my nose. I continued until I felt an overwhelming buzz. It was then that I felt strange sensations, I could feel my cheeks being pushed in and my jaw clamped, my vision turned quite blurred."

—Quoted in *Vaults of Erowid*, "Cheap and Cheerful: Erowid Experience Vaults."

"Every time kids use inhalants, they are playing Russian roulette."

—Wayland, Massachusetts, Police Department, "The Dangers of Inhalants."

I t is ironic that inhalants are considered among the most dangerous drugs, and yet they are so accessible. According to the authors of *Buzzed: The Straight Facts About the Most Used and Abused Drugs from Alcohol to Ecstasy*, "Because of their easy access to glues, gasoline, solvents, paints, and sprays, many children begin to use drugs by inhaling these common chemicals. They get a buzz, but along with that buzz comes toxic effects that would horrify any chemical safety expert."[10] Many people abuse inhalants, and workers are sometimes accidentally exposed to these chemicals.

What Are the Short-Term Risks?

The immediate side effects of inhalants vary depending upon type. Nitrites, which are frequently prescribed by doctors for heart-related problems, can result in dizziness, weakness, headaches, and even loss of consciousness if the patient makes sudden changes in his or her body position. Nitrites become much more dangerous in the short term if they are swallowed instead of inhaled. When ingested, nitrites interfere with the blood's ability to transport oxygen, and death can occur. Some nitrites are available by prescription, and others, though illegal, are sold for recreational drug use.

Nitrous oxide, an anesthetic inhalant, is also used by doctors. While it is no longer used by itself to achieve the desired anesthesia for surgery, it is used medically in combination with other anesthetics for major surgery and alone only for minor surgical procedures. Although nitrous oxide offers anesthetic benefits and has been used to treat opiate and alcohol withdrawal, it is very dangerous when used outside of clinical settings. Those who abuse nitrous oxide run the short-term risks of not getting enough oxygen and physically hurting themselves. Nitrous oxide does cause disorientation, loss of good judgment, and even unconsciousness.

While these short-term effects are serious and can be very dangerous, the short-term dangers of solvents and fuels far outweigh the dangers of other types of inhalants, such as nitrites and anesthetics. As with anesthetics, users experience dizziness, disorientation, and light-headedness. However, unlike anesthetics, the short-term effects of inhaling solvents include ringing in the ears, double vision, and abdominal pain. These effects are followed by symptoms associated with chemical depression of the central nervous system: vomiting, loss of reflexes, trouble breathing, and even death. Also, just like the short-term effects of nitrous oxide, the short-term effects of inhaling solvents include a lack of coordination and a loss of judgment. In fact, over 20 percent of deaths associated with inhalant use are from accidents, and almost 30 percent are from suicide. It is not known

> It is ironic that inhalants are considered among the most dangerous drugs, and yet they are so easily accessible.

whether inhalants affect users, causing them to become suicidal, or if depressed individuals choose inhalants as the way to end their lives. Experts such as Cynthia Kuhn, Scott Swartzwelder, and Wilkie Wilson, authors of *Buzzed*, point out that the suicides related to inhalants are probably from a combination of both scenarios, as is the case with other drugs.

> " One of the biggest short-term dangers of using fuel and solvent inhalants is called Sudden Sniffing Death Syndrome. "

One of the biggest short-term dangers of using fuel and solvent inhalants is called Sudden Sniffing Death Syndrome (SSDS). When abusers sniff substances like butane and gasoline, the heart is affected. Abnormal heart rhythms are created by chemicals that affect the heart cells that set its beating pattern, and at the same time, other heart cells experience an increased sensitivity to adrenaline. Death can result the very first time someone sniffs these types of inhalants, making them among the most dangerous "highs" possible.

Sudden Sniffing Death Syndrome and Inhalant-Related Deaths

Because the heart is so sensitive to adrenaline while using inhalants, any kind of excitement can cause death. The user has no control over this. Sometimes SSDS occurs when the user is caught using the inhalants. Other times, hallucinations can cause excitement and lead to death. Many times, it is unknown what caused the excitement. SSDS is the most common killer of inhalant abusers, and it is estimated that 22 percent of the people who die from SSDS die the first time they abuse an inhalant.

Although SSDS is generally associated with butane and propane inhaling, it can occur with other types of inhalants. For example, compressed air that is often used to clean computers has been associated with a number of SSDS cases. In 2005 a story was circulated on the Internet about a young boy in Cleveland, Ohio, who died from SSDS after inhaling compressed air. His mother, a nurse, and his father, a police officer, had never heard of people sniffing compressed air. The family pet was even a former drug-sniffing dog, so his parents thought there would be no way for drugs to ever enter their family home. The boy's mother found him the morning after he died sitting up in his bed and at first thought he was joking when he did not get up for school. When she finally went to shake him to get him to move, he was dead with the straw from the can of compressed air still in his mouth. According to his father, "The horrible part about this is there is no warning. There is no level that kills you. It's not cumulative or an overdose; it can just go randomly and terribly wrong."[11]

Sadly, this story is not rare. A 2005 Canadian Broadcast Corporation News article reported junior high school girls using compressed air to get high at school. The article goes on to explain the growing concern about this issue, as the use of compressed air for inhalant purposes has been on the rise among teens and even preteens. Compressed air, which is used to clean computers, is made of a chemical called difluoroethane, a gaseous substance that is dangerous when inhaled by humans. However, many children think that because it is called "compressed air" that it is nothing but air. Colleen Dell of the Canadian Centre on Substance Abuse in Ottawa said, "the understanding amongst the kids is that there was no gas involved, or no volatile substances involved in what they're using. They believe that they were intaking air. . . . That was completely false."[12]

> "Parents of children who have died from inhalant-related accidents also frequently work to spread the word about inhalant dangers to other parents."

Although the United States keeps no formal records on the number of deaths from SSDS or other inhalant-related deaths, media reports do frequently surface. Parents of children who have died from inhalant-related accidents also frequently work to spread the word about inhalant dangers to other parents. Researchers also point out that it can be difficult to know just how many deaths are related to inhalants because accidents happen frequently when people are under the influence of inhalants. For example, a car accident may be inhalant related, but the cause of death would not be officially listed as inhalant related. However, some research-ers have attempted to track death statistics related to inhalants. A reseacher from Texas, James Garriott, chief toxicologist in San Antonio, studied all deaths in Bexar County between 1982 and 1988 that were attributed to in-halants. According to the research, "Most of the 39 inhalant-related deaths involved teenagers, with 21 deaths occurring among people less than 20 years of age."[13]

What Are the Long-Term Risks?

Just as the short-term risks of inhalants are dangerous, the long-term risks associated with inhalant abuse and exposure are serious and can be life threatening. The long-term effects of repeated exposure to nitrous oxide, for example, can lead to problems that are similar to problems associated with vitamin B_{12} deficiency. Long-term exposure to nitrous oxide results in nerve fiber damage and, therefore, neurological problems, including weakness, tingling sensa-tions, and loss of feeling. Dentists who regularly administer nitrous oxide to their patients have experi-enced such problems.

> Most users report that it is very dif-ficult to quit using inhalants after they have used them for some time.

Long-term exposure to solvents is even more dangerous. Damage to the central nervous system is one of the biggest dangers. Long-term ex-posure to toluene, a solvent found in many glues, has been studied and found to result in damage to the cerebellum, the part of the brain associ-ated with fine movement as well as physical and procedural memory. Ad-ditionally, inhaling solvents regularly leads to damage of the heart, lungs, kidneys, and liver. The shortage of controlled research studies on long-term exposure to inhalants is due to the fact that such studies would be so dangerous to the participant.

Are Inhalants Addictive?

Most research indicates that inhalants are addictive. Most users report that it is very difficult to quit using inhalants after they have used them for some time. Also, as with alcohol use, tolerance to inhalants develops over time. This means that users have to keep inhaling larger amounts in order to feel the same effects. Though people who abuse inhalants infrequently do not experience withdrawal symptoms, those who have chronically abused the chemicals will go through a withdrawal process that includes depression, restlessness, and aggression. According to the Recovery Connection, a drug addiction treatment center Web site, "Withdrawal symptoms may include sweating, rapid pulse, hand tremors, insomnia, nausea, vomiting, physical agitation, anxiety, [and] hallucinations."[14] Inhalant users' bodies change because of the chemical use, and quitting can sometimes be difficult. According to the U.S. Drug Enforcement Administration, "A strong need to continue using inhalants has been reported among many individuals, particularly those who abuse inhalants for prolonged periods over many days. Compulsive use and a mild withdrawal syndrome can occur with long-term inhalant abuse."[15]

> "One of the biggest societal concerns about inhalants is that they seem to act as 'gateway' drugs for children."

Additionally, the National Inhalant Prevention Coalition has this to say about the addictiveness of inhalants:

> Psychological addiction and physiological dependence on inhalants does occur. . . . Many users are known to be heavily preoccupied and dependent on their favorite product or brand to experience its effects. They may be unwilling to substitute another product unless theirs is unavailable. Further, the chronic abuser is likely to require greater doses of the inhalants due to the effects on the central nervous system. Some inhalant abusers who had stopped using for a period of time reported intense inhalant cravings at unexpected times making continued sobriety very difficult.[16]

How Does Inhalant Abuse Affect Society?

For many reasons, inhalant abuse is a big concern for society. These chemicals are often used in everyday household products, so they cannot be outlawed and regulated like drugs such as cocaine and heroin. They are and will continue to be easy for children to access and experiment with. Finally, inhalants are extremely dangerous—possibly the most dangerous of all abused substances.

The 2005 National Survey on Drug Use and Health revealed that "22.7 million Americans aged 12 or older reported using inhalants at least once during their lifetimes, representing 9.4% of the population aged 12 or older. Nearly 2.2 million (0.9%) reported past year inhalant use and 611,000 (0.3%) reported past month inhalant use."[17] Although illegal drug use has declined overall in recent years, inhalants remain a significant problem for society. The Drug Abuse Warning Network estimates that during 2005, inhalants were responsible for 4,312 emergency room visits in the United States.

One of the biggest societal concerns about inhalants is that they seem to act as "gateway" drugs for children. This means that children who abuse inhalants are more likely to move on to other drugs as they get older. Although studies exploring inhalants as a clear gateway drug are ongoing, most experts agree that inhalants appear to act as a gateway drug. The Hazelden Foundation, a national nonprofit organization devoted to helping people recover from drug addiction, states, "Inhalants are referred to as a 'gateway drug' because they are often the first drugs that younger children use."[18] And according to a 2002 National Survey on Drug Use and Health, teens who use inhalants are three times more likely to use other drugs.

With all this in mind, perhaps the greatest cost to society is the reality that family after family has lost children to unnecessary deaths associated with inhalant abuse. The cost of losing a child or other young family member can never be measured. One personal story as reported on the U.S. Drug Enforcement Administration's Web site tells of the impact of this loss: "I lost my 13-year-old brother to inhalant abuse. He died in my arms at the county hospital, and there was nothing that the doctors could do. I was the one who took him to the hospital after some of his friends had a 'sniffing party.' He sniffed his way to his own death. He didn't know that inhalants could kill him."[19]

What Are the Risks of Inhalant Abuse?

66**This affinity for brain regions associated with reward and pleasure, as well as the quick uptake and clearance, may help to explain why inhalants are so commonly abused.**99

—Madina Gerasimov, quoted in "Brain-Imaging Study Offers Clues to Inhalant Abuse—Huffing," *U.S. Department of Energy Research News*, April 2002.

Gerasimov is a chemist at the U.S. Department of Energy's Brookhaven National Laboratory.

66**I began to have hallucinations inside my body. I felt like an air bubble was running through my bloodstream, and my heart was beginning to turn inside out. This freaked me out; I stopped huffing.**99

—Jordan, "Inhalants-Gasoline," Childhood Memories Relived, Erowid, 2002. www.erowid.org.

Jordan had been using various drugs for one year when he wrote about his experiences with inhalants on Erowid's Web site.

* Editor's Note: While the definition of a primary source can be narrowly or broadly defined, for the purposes of Compact Research, a primary source consists of: 1) results of original research presented by an organization or researcher; 2) eyewitness accounts of events, personal experience, or work experience; 3) first-person editorials offering pundits' opinions; 4) government officials presenting political plans and/or policies; 5) representatives of organizations presenting testimony or policy.

66If you ask me, all inhalants are a huge waste of my precious time! I get so sad when I hear about people sniffing these things. They just don't know how they are hurting themselves.99

—Girl Power! "Body F/X: Inhalants," 2007. www.girlpower.gov.

Girl Power! is the national public education campaign sponsored by the U.S. Department of Health and Human Services to help encourage and motivate 9- to 13-year-old girls to make the most of their lives.

66What used to be called huffing has now become dusting. What used to be a novelty is now a serious problem.99

—SporTech Inc., "Waiting to Inhale: These Days, Teens Are Huffing, Not Puffing," editorial, September 2005. www.sport-tech.org.

SporTech Inc. is a nationally recognized program designed to increase awareness and prevent use of drugs, especially in the area of competitive sports. It has been the recipient of a presidential commendation for drug education.

66'Harmless' fun killed our son. We talked openly with Ricky about the dangers of drugs and alcohol but we *never* warned him about the dangers of inhalants.99

—Diane Stem, "Ricky Joe Stem Jr.—*OUR SON*," Ricky Joe Stem Memorial. http://hometown.aol.com.

Diane and her husband, who lost their child to "huffing," are advocates for educating families about the tragedy that follows when children use seemingly innocent household products to get high.

66Those who live through their first huffing experience are in danger of dying each time they try it again.99

—Patrick S. Pasquariello Jr., "Leaving in a Huff: Inhalants Can Cause Immediate Death," *Children's Health Tip of the Day*, Children's Hospital of Philadelphia, 2007.

Pasquariello is director of both the Diagnostic Center and the Spina Bifida Program of the Special Care and Family Medicine divisions of the Children's Hospital of Philadephia.

66Laughing gas is by no means a risk-free drug; when used outside of a controlled medical setting it can be dangerous. Nitrous oxide replaces oxygen in the lungs . . . it can lead to fatal asphyxiation.99

—Martin Barnes, "Purge on 'Lethal' Laughing Gas in Clubs and Bars," *Times* (London), March 2007. www.timesonline.co.uk.

Barnes is the chief executive of the charity Drug-Scope, a nonprofit informational organization in Britain dedicated to increasing awareness of the dangers of drug abuse.

66An important lesson I learned after treatment was that my supposed friends only liked me when I was high. I also learned I didn't like me when I was high.99

—Megan Hakeman, "The Story of a Teen Girl's Huffing Addiction," March 2005. www.drugfree.org.

Hakeman turned to inhalants after a traumatic event in her life that she did not think she could handle.

66Drug education at school was completely counter-productive, consisting of being told, at age 14, to 'do a project on drugs' with no instructions. John decided to research glue sniffing by trying it.99

—Mother of a teenager, quoted in Roslyn Phillips, "Substance Abuse in Australian Communities," submission to the House of Representatives' Standing Committee on Family and Community Affairs, Parliament House, June 2000.

A mother whose teenage son was apprehended by a teacher for sniffing glue is quoted by Phillips in her report to the Australian House of Representatives. Phillips is the research officer with Festival of Light Australia, a nonprofit organization.

66Some of the children spend every waking moment in a drug-addled daze, 'huffing' an industrial paint to get high. Their faces are smeared with a sparkling, shimmering, silvery poison.**99**

—National Public Radio, *Children Underground,* review, 2002. www.npr.org.

National Public Radio is a not-for-profit producer and distributor of noncommercial programming. In its review of the Oscar-nominated film *Children Underground*, NPR describes the toll "huffing" has taken on the already tragic lives of discarded Romanian street children.

66In this whole world of good smells and bad smells, inhalants are a set of chemicals that can make life stink.**99**

—Jennifer James, "Inhalants: Why to Pass on Gas," Do It Now Foundation, 2002.

Jennifer James is one of the authors of a series of e-pamphlets from the Do It Now Foundation written to offer friendly, down-to-earth, and accessible information about drugs, behavior, and healthy choices.

66Before I reached the age of twelve I was huffing paint and gasoline, sniffing glue and whiteout and setting things on fire. I was also having more seizures than ever.**99**

—Don, "Heroes Among Us," Epilepsy Foundation, 2006. www.epilepsyfoundation.org.

Don has volunteered to share his struggles of living with injury-induced epilepsy. With an alcoholic father as a model, Don turned to inhalants to cope and then moved on to other drugs, both illegal and prescription, before he finally sought help.

Facts and Illustrations

What Are the Risks of Inhalant Abuse?

- Evidence suggests that **toluene** harms developing fetuses by affecting the brain's glial cells. These cells hold the brain's neurons together, provide nutrients, and take away waste products.

- Another form of inhaling is called **"fire breathing"**—filling the mouth with butane and blowing it out over a lighter or other flame source. While the effect may be spectacular, it can also be deadly. Serious damage to the lungs can occur.

- An unexpected source of **lead poisoning** in children comes from inhaling gasoline products. The lead from the fuel vapors gets in through the lungs and accumulates in the body. Major neurological damage can occur, resulting in impaired learning and even death.

- Glue and gasoline can cause **uncontrolled spasms** and ultimately damage bone marrow, leading to pernicious anemia. Also, extended use can lead to leaking bladder and anal sphincters.

- Although death from **sniffing glue** is usually related to insufficient oxygen to the brain, either because of too little oxygen in the blood or by the plastic bag covering the head, heart failure can also result in sudden death if a person exercises or tries to run right after sniffing.

- Convulsions can result from even short-term abuse of solvents such as toluene. In a **brain scan**, the sudden onset of epilepsy in a young

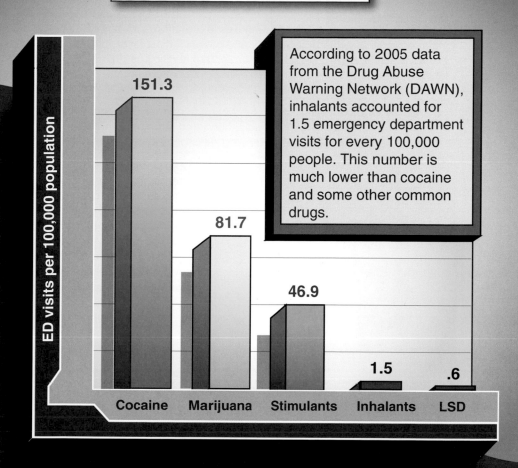

Drug-Related Emergency Department Visits for 2005

According to 2005 data from the Drug Abuse Warning Network (DAWN), inhalants accounted for 1.5 emergency department visits for every 100,000 people. This number is much lower than cocaine and some other common drugs.

ED visits per 100,000 population

151.3 — Cocaine
81.7 — Marijuana
46.9 — Stimulants
1.5 — Inhalants
.6 — LSD

Source: Drug Abuse Warning Network, U.S. Department of Health and Human Services, "National Estimates of Drug-Related Emergency Department Visits," 2005.

boy was found to be from wedge-shaped areas of damage in his brain from glue sniffing.

• Nearly **33 percent** of adolescents who "huff" start by using glue, shoe polish, or paint thinner. Gasoline and lighter fluid follow at a close second.

Inhalants Damage the Brain, Muscle, and Bone Marrow

(A) Brain The chemicals abused by inhalant users affect different parts of the brain, producing a variety of sensory and psychological disorders. Many inhalants are thought to dissolve the protective myelin sheath that surrounds neurons—brain cells—resulting in cell death (see brain diagram).

(B) Cerebral Cortex Cellular death here causes permanent personality changes, memory impairment, hallucinations and learning disabilities.

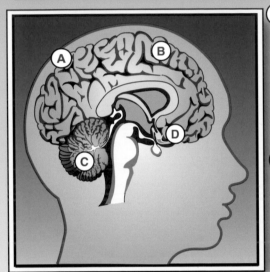

(C) Cerebellum This is the center that controls balance and coordination. Inhalant-related damage results in loss of coordination and slurred speech. Chronic abusers experience tremors and uncontrollable shaking.

(D) Ophthalmic Nerve Toluene may affect this nerve, causing sight disorders.

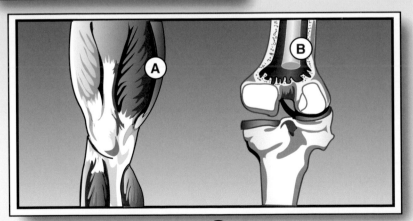

(A) Muscle Chronic inhalant abuse can lead to muscle wasting and reduced muscle tone and strength.

(B) Bone Marrow Benzene, a component of gasoline, has been shown to cause leukemia.

Source: National Inhalant Prevention Coalition, "Damage Inhalants Can Do to the Body & Brain," 2007. www.inhalants.org.

Inhalants Damage the Body

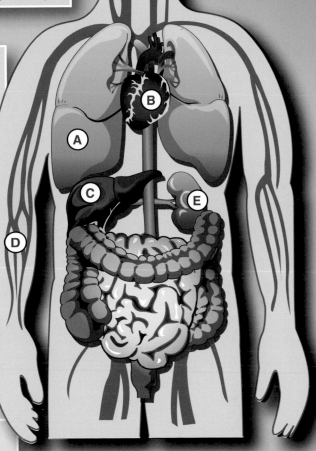

A **Lungs** Repeated use of spray paint as an inhalant can cause lung damage.

B **Heart** Abuse of inhalants can result in "sudden sniffing death syndrome." This is due to a sudden and unexpected disturbance of the heart's rhythm. All inhalants can produce sudden sniffing death syndrome.

C **Liver** Halogenated compounds like trichloroethylene (a component of aerosol paints and correction fluid) have been linked to damage of this organ.

D **Blood** Some substances like nitrites and methylene chloride (paint thinner) chemically block the oxygen-carrying capacity of the blood.

E **Kidney** Inhalants containing toluene impair the kidney's ability to control the amount of acid in the blood. This is reversible when toluene leaves the body, but, in the long-term, kidney stones may develop.

Source: National Inhalant Prevention Coalition. "Damage Inhalants Can Do to the Body & Brain." 2007. www.inhalants.org.

- The common causes of death from inhalant abuse include asphyxiation, suffocation, **choking on vomit**, or fatal injuries from car accidents either as a driver or passenger. Sudden Sniffing Death Syndrome is a particular result of abusing butane or propane and even chemicals found in aerosol cans.

- There is a correlation between **abusing inhalants** and overall problems, especially in school. Adolescents that "huff" tend to have failing grades, probably due to memory loss and other learning problems linked to nerve damage. They also are absent more often and **apathetic** in general.

- Research has shown that **chronic use of inhalants** such as toluene set up the brain to be much more responsive to other drugs, such as cocaine.

How Does Inhalant Abuse Affect Society?

❝Solvents, including gasoline, sprays, glues, paints, cleaning fluids, and everything else, were never intended for human use. [We] consider these among the most toxic substances used for drug recreation, and we believe that they should never be used by anyone under any circumstances, especially children.❞

—Cynthia Kuhn, Scott Swartzwelder, and Wilkie Wilson, *Buzzed: The Straight Facts About the Most Used and Abused Drugs from Alcohol to Ecstasy.*

❝The highest incidence of use is among 10 to 12 year old children with rates of use declining with age. Parents worry about alcohol, tobacco, and drug use but may be unaware of the hazards associated with products found throughout their homes.❞

—U.S. Drug Enforcement Administration, *Drugs of Abuse,* "Chapter 9: Inhalants."

Inhalant abuse occurs in all age groups and across all socioeconomic classes, but abuse is much more prevalent among groups of people who cannot afford other drugs. Inhalants are cheap; therefore, they are more commonly used by young children and poor people without any disposable income to buy drugs. Abuse of these chemicals presents problems for all of us, however. Inhalant abuse is not limited to the United

States, as the United Kingdom, Canada, Australia, and other nations all report inhalant abuse problems, particularly among children. Additionally, developing nations struggle with inhalant abuse, as inhalants are often the only "high" people can afford. According to Glen R. Hanson, Peter J. Venturelli, and Annette E. Fleckenstein, authors of *Drugs and Society*, "The problem of inhalant abuse is not unique to the United States. According to research data reported by the National Institute on Drug Abuse (NIDA), inhalant abuse is a worldwide concern. Low prices and easy access make inhalants as problematic in Asia, Africa, and Latin America as the United States."[20] Research studies in Africa, such as the World Youth Report in 2003, indicate that in some African communities 60 percent of the youths use inhalants. The same report indicates that inhalants are also a significant problem among poor aboriginal groups in Australia. In the United Kingdom, researchers tracked 2,100 deaths associated with inhalants between 1971 and 2003. Half of these deaths occurred in children under the age of 18, and the youngest to die was a 7-year-old.

> " Inhalants are cheap; therefore, they are more commonly used by young children and poor people without any disposable income to buy drugs. "

Clearly, abuse of these chemicals is something to be concerned about. Abuse has continued to be a significant issue in the United States, even as use of other drugs has declined in recent years. Most agree that there is much work to be done when it comes to preventing inhalant abuse, but the practical uses of these chemicals in our everyday lives have made them difficult to control. Undoubtedly, inhalants will continue to be a problem in our society and others throughout the world.

Why Are Inhalants Legal?

Inhalants are not regulated under the U.S. Controlled Substances Act because they are found in products that people use every day at work and at home. People are abusing substances that were never meant to be breathed by humans. For example, people abuse the chemicals used in glues, but it is impractical for the government to make glue illegal.

Our lives would certainly be more difficult in many ways without these products. Therefore, these products have and probably will continue to remain legal.

What Attempts Have Been Made to Regulate Inhalants?

This does not mean, however, that efforts have not been made to limit access of these chemicals to children. Inhalants may be legal, but because of the dangers and high number of children abusing these chemicals, laws have been passed that attempt to make these chemicals at least a little more difficult for children to access. According to the U.S. Drug Enforcement Administration:

> Although not regulated under the Controlled Substances Act (CSA), many state legislatures have attempted to deter youth who buy legal products to get high by placing restrictions on the sale of these products to minors. As reported by the National Conference of State Legislatures, by 2000, 38 States had adopted laws preventing the sale, use, and/ or distribution to minors of various products commonly abused as inhalants. Some States have introduced fines, incarceration, or mandatory treatment for the sale, distribution, use, and/or possession of inhalable chemicals.[21]

Many states have passed laws limiting the sale of items that contain chemicals frequently abused as inhalants. For example, in New Jersey it is illegal to sell to minors any product containing chlorofluorocarbon, which is used as a refrigerant. In New Mexico it is illegal to sell minors model glue, aerosol spray, and any intoxicating chemicals. And in California, it is illegal to sell toluene, materials containing toluene, and nitrous oxide to minors. Many states that have not passed laws prohibiting the sale of

> " Inhalants are not regulated under the U.S. Controlled Substances Act because they are found in products that people use every day at work and at home. "

commonly abused inhalant substances to minors have at least passed laws making it illegal to "inhale certain compounds for intoxication."[22]

It is important to note, however, that these laws are very difficult to enforce and that most experts agree that the best way to control inhalant abuse is through educational efforts. According to Sophia F. Dziegielewski, author of *Understanding Substance Addictions*, "Forty states have laws limiting or prohibiting the sale or use of inhalants to minors, but these laws are difficult to enforce. The deterrence of inhalant abuse requires education about the signs of use and harmful effects."[23]

> As with many other illegally abused substances, a strong correlation exists between inhalant abuse and crime, in part because of the aggressive behaviors demonstrated by inhalant abusers.

The United States is not the only country to struggle with regulating inhalants. In Australia, where inhalant abuse is also a significant problem, no federal laws prohibit the use or possession of volatile substances. Communities in South and Western Australia have passed local laws making it illegal to sniff inhalants for intoxication, but these laws are certainly difficult to enforce. According to the Australian Drug Foundation, "While some inhalants are restricted, most inhalants are common household products, so it is not practical to make them illegal. It is also unlikely that this would help protect young people from harm. However, it is illegal for retailers to sell products to someone if they believe that they are to be used for inhaling."[24]

What Are the Costs of Inhalant Abuse?

According to the National Inhalant Prevention Coalition (NIPC), the costs of inhalant abuse, though sometimes difficult to quantify, are high for society. One way inhalant abuse costs society is by "culturizing" future generations for more inhalant abuse. Essentially, according to the NIPC, "The community provides a base within which all other socialization occurs. Consequently, the community maintains very strong effects by itself. When children in a community use inhalants heavily it can suggest sniffing to the next age cohort as they grow up as well as legitimize it with their peers."[25] Additionally, crime is an issue, as is academic success.

Crime

As with many other illegally abused substances, a strong correlation exists between inhalant abuse and crime, in part because of the aggressive behaviors demonstrated by inhalant abusers. According to the National Inhalant Prevention Coalition, "Chronic inhalant abusers often have significant levels of psychopathology, aggressive behavior, violence and they engage in a wide variety of deviant and delinquent activities."[26] The Australian Institute of Criminology also points to surveys indicating that 49 percent of young offenders in Australia had used inhalants in their lifetimes.

American research into the behavior of incarcerated individuals reveals a strong, clear connection between drug abuse and criminal behavior. Although inhalants are not as prevalent as other drugs in these research studies, they are an issue for some people in both state and federal prisons. According to Christopher J. Mumola and Jennifer C. Karberg from the U.S. Department of Justice's Bureau of Justice Statistics, in 2004, 4.5 percent of individuals incarcerated in state prisons revealed that they had regularly abused inhalants before committing their crimes. At the federal level, 3 percent of inmates surveyed said they had abused inhalants regularly before committing their crimes.[27]

> While many private companies provide some funding for educational programs, government agencies still bear significant costs.

Education

In terms of education, inhalant abuse costs society money in two ways. First, inhalant abuse among teens and preteens leads to serious struggles with schoolwork. The National Inhalant Prevention Coalition reports, "Inhalant abusers usually have educational problems. They usually experience high truancy and dropout rates, problems with school authorities and poor school performance. Young inhalant abusers demonstrate less liking for school as well as school adjustment problems."[28] This poor school performance presents problems not only for the young inhalant abusers but also for the greater society. These students are less likely to succeed in their education and, therefore, are less likely to be gainfully employed.

The federal, state, and local educational campaigns to prevent inhalant abuse are also costly to society. D.A.R.E., the Drug Abuse Resistance Education program, costs around $750,000,000 per year, according to Glenn Levant, the D.A.R.E. executive director. Of course, not all of this money goes to inhalant education alone; nevertheless the expense of inhalant abuse education is included in D.A.R.E.'s program. While many private companies provide some funding for educational programs, government agencies still bear significant costs. Nonprofit organizations that receive some funding from government agencies spend millions on public service announcements to run in television and radio markets all over the country. One example of these organizations' efforts to educate the American public about the dangers of inhalant abuse is the creation of National Inhalants Prevention Awareness Week.

National Inhalants Prevention Awareness Week

National Inhalants Prevention Awareness Week (NIPAW) was created by the National Inhalant Prevention Coalition to educate Americans, community by community, about the dangers and signs of inhalant abuse. NIPAW is media based, and local communities are encouraged to get involved. According to the National Inhalant Prevention Coalition:

> NIPAW is designed to increase understanding about the use and risks of inhalant involvement. It is an inclusive program that involves youth, schools, media, police departments, health organizations, civic groups and more. It has proven to be an effective means of mobilizing communities to reduce inhalant use. Almost 2,000 organizations and individuals from 46 states participated in the last NIPAW campaign.[29]

A great example of money well spent, this event, taking place the third week of March every year, has proven successful. The National Inhalant Prevention Coalition reports positive results:

Results from Texas, where extensive state-wide NIPAW campaigns have been conducted, have been remarkable. Between 1992 and 1994, there was a reduction of more than 30 percent in elementary school inhalant use and a reduction of more than 20 percent at the high school level (based on state agency surveys of more than 176,000 students). This translates into over 100,000 students who may have used inhalants but didn't.[30]

The costs of inhalant abuse are clearly high for society, but efforts are being made to control inhalant abuse, which, in turn, helps control these costs.

Primary Source Quotes*

How Does Inhalant Abuse Affect Society?

66Students want to hear from people who've been through it [drug abuse]. But the federal government won't fund that kind of program. They don't want kids to think you can make it through.99

—Jordan Horowitz, quoted in Joanne Jacobs, editorial, *San Jose Mercury News*, November 13, 1995.

Horowitz is an analyst at the Southwest Regional Laboratory in Los Alamitos, California, and spent more than three years conducting research on drug abuse resistance education programs in California.

66Elementary school children no longer associate huffing exclusively with the big bad wolf.99

—Mary Galbraith, "Huffing: A Deadly Rising Trend for Teens, Pre-Teens," *Hilltop Times*, July 1999.

Galbraith is a staff writer for the *Hilltop Times*, a local newspaper in Utah.

* Editor's Note: While the definition of a primary source can be narrowly or broadly defined, for the purposes of Compact Research, a primary source consists of: 1) results of original research presented by an organization or researcher; 2) eyewitness accounts of events, personal experience, or work experience; 3) first-person editorials offering pundits' opinions; 4) government officials presenting political plans and/or policies; 5) representatives of organizations presenting testimony or policy.

Primary Source Quotes

66I'll never stop sniffing gas.99

—Philip Rich, CBC Archives, November 2000. http://archives.cbc.ca.

Philip, age 11, is a member of the Labrador Innu, a native community in Newfoundland. Philip, along with his friends and siblings, continually inhales gasoline even though his brother Charles burned to death at age 11 while sniffing gasoline by candlelight.

66Every weekday I catch myself sitting on the living room couch at 2:30 in the afternoon, waiting to see him get off the bus. I know Kyle is in heaven but I can't help wonder if I died and went to hell.99

—Jeff Williams, quoted in *Cleveland Plain Dealer*, March 2005.

Williams is a police officer. His son Kyle died at age 14 from "dusting." In his grief Williams talked to the press and circulated an e-mail statement to warn children and parents about the dangers of inhaling compressed air.

66[I was] shocked the first time I saw an adult watch a child walking by with his head in a garbage bag without going over and taking it away.99

—Eric Kennedy, "Who Will Help the Kids?" *Worth-a-Look: Interesting Articles on the Frontier of Public Policy*, 2005.

Kennedy is a social worker and supervisor of the Southeast Child and Family Services office in Paulingassi, outside of Winnipeg, Canada. He is determined to stop the abuse of inhalants and alcohol in his small community.

66We are unwitting pushers in our own homes. They're under every kitchen sink, they're under our bathroom sinks.99

—Susan Wilson Tucker, "Inhalant Abuse Kills with Little Public Attention," CNN, March 1999. www.cnn.com.

Tucker is the mother of a young girl who was killed while riding in a car driven by a friend who had been abusing inhalants. Tucker has worked tirelessly to convince the Georgia General Assembly to pass a bill making driving under the influence of inhalants illegal.

66You could have knocked me over with a feather. We are a decent family. I've never even had a cigarette in my mouth. How could my teenage daughter be a huffing addict?99

—Joan Hakeman, "My Daughter's Huffing Addiction," Partnership for a Drug-Free America. www.drugfree.org.

Hakeman never suspected her daughter was the victim of stress and peer pressure. She volunteered to tell her story so that other parents may recognize the warning signs of inhalant abuse as well as warn young people about the dangers of this "cheap" high.

66Loving, precious young man and huffing victim. Tyler was experimenting; I am sure he did not know it could kill him. He had no intention of leaving us that dreadful day.99

—Michel Townsend, 2007. *Drugfree.org* memorials. www.drugfree.org.

Townsend posted the events leading up to the death of her 14-year-old son, who decided to take a huff or two before dinner.

66As law enforcement efforts make illicit drugs more costly and difficult to obtain, more of our nation's youth will turn to 'legal' inhalant abuse for the 'high' that they crave.99

—Clark Staten, "Youths Die by Inhaling Household Substances," EmergencyNet News Service, 2006. www.emergency.com.

Staten is the executive director of the Emergency Response and Research Institute, based in Chicago, Illinois. This agency is dedicated to the dissemination of information about society's challenges.

❝Let's not forget the media can also play a very positive role in influencing the attitudes of our young people about the unacceptability of using drugs. The Partnership for a Drug-Free America has proven that over and over again. . . . These messages are working to change attitudes. They can make a difference.❞

—William J. Clinton, "Select Quotes About the Partnership," Partnership for a Drug-Free America, 2006. www.drugfree.org.

Clinton was the forty-second president of the United States, serving from 1993 to 2001.

❝While overall drug use among young people has declined substantially over the past four years, we must not lose our focus. Inhalant abuse remains a dangerous and potentially deadly behavior that parents need to be aware of. Too many parents are not aware that inhalants are as popular among middle school students as marijuana. We encourage all parents to learn the signs of inhalant abuse and to monitor their teens.❞

—John Walters, quoted in Substance Abuse and Mental Health Services Administration, "1.8 Million Youth Initiate Inhalant Abuse in Three Years," 2006. www.samhsa.gov.

Walters is director of the White House Office of National Drug Control Policy, a federal organization charged with setting drug policy for the United States.

❝Sniffing gasoline or paint is a grubby, dirty, cheap way to get high.❞

—Frederick G. Hofmann, *Handbook on Drug and Alcohol Abuse*, 1975.

Hofmann is a professor emeritus of psychopharmacology at Columbia University. He has published several editions *of Handbook on Drug and Alcohol Abuse* and many scholarly articles on the neurological and behavioral effects of drugs.

Facts and Illustrations

How Does Inhalant Abuse Affect Society?

- According to the most recent National Household Survey on Drug Abuse conducted by the Substance Abuse and Mental Health Services Administration, **16.7 million persons** surveyed had abused inhalants at some time during their lives, compared with only 6.4 million who had used Ecstasy.

- **Fetal solvent syndrome** is very similar to fetal alcohol syndrome. Babies have low birth weights, small head sizes, disfigured faces, and problems with muscle tone.

- Many states are **enacting laws** that make it illegal to inhale substances for intoxication.

- An estimated **1.1 million children** between ages 12 and 17 use inhalants to get high, and for the first time a slightly higher percentage of girls than boys are huffing household products and starting younger than their male counterparts.

- When the Substance Abuse and Mental Health Services Administration last reported on **inhalant use** in 2002, only 4.1 percent of girls used inhalants compared to 4.6 percent of boys. In 2005 nearly 5 percent of girls used inhalants, while just 4.2 percent of boys reported huffing.

- Only **4 percent** of parents of middle school students believe their

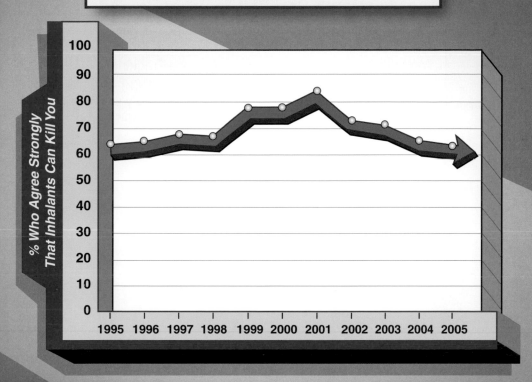

Percent of Teens Who Strongly Agree That Inhalants Can Kill You Is Down

According to a 2005 Partnership Attitude Tracking Study conducted by the Partnership for a Drug-Free America, 64 percent of teens surveyed strongly agree that inhalants can kill you. This number is down 19 percent from 2001.

Source: The 2005 Partnership Attitude Tracking Study (PATS), the Partnership for a Drug-Free America. www.drugfree.org.

children have tried inhalants, but **25 percent** of middle school students has actually tried them at least once.

- Inhalant abusers are much more likely to be arrested for virtually every type and category of **delinquent activity**, including crimes against property and violent offenses.

- If **nitrous oxide** is mixed with room air rather than pure oxygen, severe depletion of oxygen to the brain will result.

- Between the 1995 peak in **inhalant abuse** and 2001, teen perceptions of the risks associated with inhalant abuse increased significantly,

Seventy-Seven Percent of Teens Strongly Agree That Inhalants Can Cause Brain Damage

According to a 2005 Partnership Attitude Tracking Study conducted by the Partnership for a Drug-Free America, 77 percent of teens surveyed strongly agree that inhalants can cause brain damage. This number is down 9 percent from 2001.

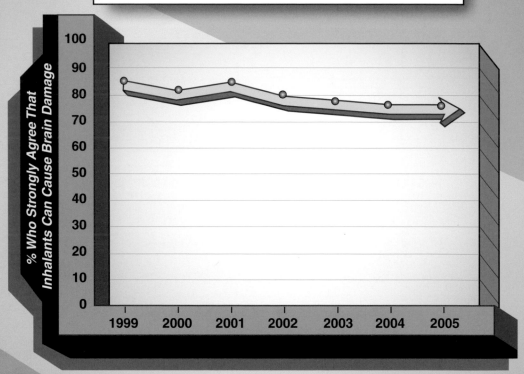

Source: The 2005 Partnership Attitude Tracking Study (PATS), the Partnership for a Drug-Free America. www.drugfree.org.

from 64 percent to 79 percent. Correspondingly, **teen inhalant abuse** declined from 23 percent to 18 percent during that same period.

- The **effects of inhalants** are immediate, as opposed to the effects of some other drugs, which can take up to 20 or 30 minutes to be felt. Some experts believe the instant "gratification" of inhalants may be a reason they are so frequently abused by young children.

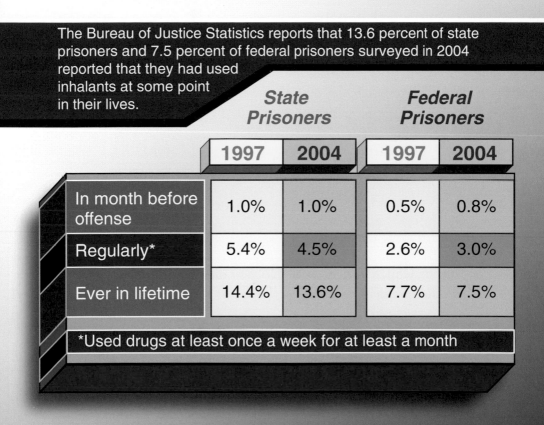

Percent of Prisoners Reporting Inhalant Use in 1997 and 2004

The Bureau of Justice Statistics reports that 13.6 percent of state prisoners and 7.5 percent of federal prisoners surveyed in 2004 reported that they had used inhalants at some point in their lives.

	State Prisoners		Federal Prisoners	
	1997	2004	1997	2004
In month before offense	1.0%	1.0%	0.5%	0.8%
Regularly*	5.4%	4.5%	2.6%	3.0%
Ever in lifetime	14.4%	13.6%	7.7%	7.5%

*Used drugs at least once a week for at least a month

Source: Office of National Drug Control Policy, "Drug Facts: Inhalants," 2007. www.whitehousedrugpolicy.gov.

Percentage of High School Students Who Used Inhalants, by Ethnicity

According to a 2005 survey from the Department of Health and Human Services Centers for Disease Control and Prevention, white high school students had the highest percentages for lifetime inhalant use with 13.4 percent. Whites were followed closely by Hispanics, with 13 percent.

Lifetime Inhalant Use

Race/Ethnicity	%
White	13.4
Black	6.8
Hispanic	13.0

Source: *Morbidity and Mortality Weekly Report*, Department of Health and Human Services Centers for Disease Control and Prevention, 2006.

- In the United Kingdom **50 percent** of all deaths associated with inhalants are of children under the age of 18.

- Risk of drug use and **binge drinking** among college students was found in one study to be strongly associated with **early inhalant use**, more so than with early mairjuana use.

- In 2006 a man was convicted of **killing his mother** after drinking beer and sniffing glue. According to the man's attorney, the man could not explain why he killed his mother, as he loved her very much.

How Can Inhalant Use Be Controlled?

> **" I actually got the idea of sniffing gas from my High School drug program. I never heard of it, but the book said that it would induce hallucinations, so, I was in to try it out. I wanted to know what it means to hallucinate. Basically, I would remove the cap from a gas can and take a few very slow and deep breaths with my mouth to the opening. The air was flowing through it because there is a little air release valve cap on the top. "**
>
> —Cobra, "A Few Huffs from Death."

> **" The continuing existence of this type of drug abuse among children and adolescents, especially given the dangers of inhalant use, underscores the need for continued concern and increased efforts to eradicate the problem. "**
>
> —Sophia F. Dziegielewski, *Understanding Substance Addictions: Assessment and Intervention.*

While controversies exist about how best to control inhalant abuse, most experts agree that education is the best way to prevent it. But even this assumption has proven controversial at times. D.A.R.E., the national Drug Abuse Resistance Education program, works to educate children in the schools about the dangers of alcohol, tobacco, and drugs, including inhalants. According to a 1991 research study published in the medical journal *Health Education Research*, while D.A.R.E. programs raised awareness about the costs of using alcohol, tobacco, and drugs, these programs had little impact on students' decisions

> According to a 1991 research study published in the medical journal *Health Education Research*, while D.A.R.E. programs raised awareness about the costs of using alcohol, tobacco, and drugs, these programs had little impact on students' decisions to use these substances.

to use these substances. The researchers conducting and reporting on their study, Christopher Ringwalt, Susan T. Ennett, and Kathleen D. Holt from the School of Public Health at the University of North Carolina, say, "DARE demonstrated no effect on adolescents' use of alcohol, cigarettes or inhalants, or on their future intentions to use these substances."[31]

Nevertheless, education remains the most effective and practical solution to the inhalant abuse issue. Some positive results have occurred from these efforts. A 2001 study surveying parents, teachers, principals, and over 1,500 D.A.R.E. students indicated that these people felt the program was effective. D.A.R.E.'s Web site refers to research on the program's effectiveness from sociologist Joseph Donnermeyer of Ohio State University:

> Teachers surveyed gave an over-all rating of the D.A.R.E. program in the good to excellent range of 97%. D.A.R.E. effectively teaches children to say no to drugs and violence according to 92.8% of parents surveyed. 94.5% of parents recommend the D.A.R.E. program be continued based on their child's experience. 86% of principals surveyed believe students will be less likely to use substances after the D.A.R.E. program.[32]

Recent survey data from the Monitoring the Future study presents both successes and continuing struggles in educating youth about the dangers of inhalants. On the positive side, the percent of eighth and twelfth graders who said they had used inhalants in the past 12 months went down in 2006 from 2004. On the negative side, however, the percentage of students who see using inhalants once or twice as a "great risk" is down as well. This raises important questions about the success of educational campaigns or the need for more.

What Laws Exist?

No federal laws exist in the United States to control distribution and use of inhalants. Likewise, it is not an offense to use inhalants anywhere in Europe. In the United States Massachusetts and some other states require retailers to check the ID of any customer purchasing certain inhalants, such as glue, and then keep a record of the sale for possible police inspection. And in Texas it is illegal for anyone to possess, sell, or buy "abusable volatile chemicals." However, the definition of volatile chemicals makes them difficult to regulate. Certainly, Texas has not outlawed glue or canned air, so what does "abusable" mean? This is part of the problem with inhalant abuse. Control of the distribution of inhalants is next to impossible, and regulation of who smells what is even more difficult.

> The Virginia Department of Education points out that one good way to control inhalant abuse legally is to require manufacturers of products with abuse potential to add irritants or stinging vapors to their products.

The Virginia Department of Education points out that one good way to control inhalant abuse legally is to require manufacturers of products with abuse potential to add irritants or stinging vapors to their products. This would make abuse of these products difficult if not impossible. Some companies have done this, but it has been on a voluntary basis. For example, a model-glue company in Illinois added oil of mustard to its glue as a deterrent to sniffing, which has proven to be successful. And a bitterant was recently added to a popular compressed air product to discourage inhalant abuse. However, so far no federal laws have been passed to require all companies to take similar actions, so nonlegal methods of control remain the only option.

What Are Nonlegal Methods of Control?

Nonlegal methods of control have taken shape in national educational campaigns designed to inform both parents and children of the dangers of inhalant abuse. In the early 1990s inhalant abuse jumped significantly among junior high and high school students, peaking around 1994 and 1995. At that time massive educational campaigns were launched in the media and in the schools, and results were positive. The percentage of eighth graders who had used inhalants during their lifetimes dropped from 21.6 percent in 1995 to 15.8 percent in 2003. Percentages also declined for high school students. The number of 10th graders who reported using inhalants during their lifetimes peaked at 19.3 percent in 1996 and had dropped to 12.4 percent by 2004. But then an interesting and disturbing trend appeared; after 2004, the percentages began to climb again. The big question was why.

According to the Partnership for a Drug-Free America, a phenomenon called "generational forgetting" is a factor in drug education. Groups like the Partnership for a Drug-Free America and the National Inhalants Prevention Coalition must work constantly to educate children about the dangers of inhalants. The numbers indicate that when the educational campaigns ease up, even a little, the number of children abusing inhalants goes up as well. President and CEO of the Partnership for a Drug-Free America, Steve Pasierb explains, "Today's middle school kids weren't exposed to the public-education campaigns and community efforts of the 1990's. This is a new generation of kids that needs our help."[33]

> **With each new generation of children, a new generation of parents may be completely unaware of the dangers of inhalant abuse.**

But children are not the only ones who require constant education. With each new generation of children, a new generation of parents may be completely unaware of the dangers of inhalant abuse. Many parents have never even heard of sniffing household chemicals to get high. One young boy who died from sniffing compressed air had a father who was a police officer and a mother who was a nurse. Neither one of them had ever heard of "sniffing" or "huffing." This is a great concern for organizations like the Partnership for a Drug-Free America, because parents are often the best and only line of defense when it comes to inhalant abuse.

Kim Manlove is a parent who lost his son David to inhalant abuse in 2001. Since then, Manlove works with his wife to share David's story in order to educate parents on this issue. "Our hope is that by sharing our story and David's struggles with substance and inhalant abuse, we can help other families open their eyes to the possibility that their kids might be engaging in very risky behaviors, that inhalant abuse is very real and very dangerous."[34] Indeed, recent surveys indicate that parents do need to be more aware and more vigilant when it comes to inhalant abuse. According to a 1995 survey sponsored by the Partnership for a Drug-Free America, only 5 percent of parents believed their child had ever abused inhalants. During that same year, according to the Monitoring the Future survey from the University of Michigan, 17.1 percent of eighth graders reported having used inhalants some time in their life.

> **According to several organizations who work to prevent inhalant abuse, such as the National Inhalant Prevention Coalition, parents should start talking to their children about the dangers of inhalant chemicals at a very early age.**

Watching for Signs and Symptoms

Research indicates that parents are the best people to prevent inhalant abuse, so once parents are aware of the problems with inhalants, they have to do something about it. According to several organizations who work to prevent inhalant abuse, such as the National Inhalant Prevention Coalition, parents should start talking to their children about the dangers of inhalant chemicals at a very early age. Because these dangerous chemicals exist in everyday products that can be found in any home, children have access at very early ages. The Virginia Department of Education starts educational programs in their public schools as early as kindergarten. The programs for the youngest students focus on teaching children the basic difference between safe and unsafe substances. In the final lesson in the kindergarten through third grade program, students are asked to look at pictures of items such as insect spray and paint as well as roses and bananas and to place X marks over the items that are not safe to smell. The education program is more advanced for older students, but the emphasis is that it is important to start talking to children about inhalants at an early age.

One of the biggest parts of all inhalant abuse education campaigns is teaching people, especially parents and teachers but students as well, what to look for in terms of signs and symptoms of inhalant abuse. According to Isabel Burk, author of the "Inhalant Prevention Resource Guide" for the Virginia Department of Education:

> Early intervention is critical for the health and safety of the inhalant abuser. Students who huff or sniff regularly tend to exhibit behavior typical of drug abusers: acting out behavior, drop in grades, withdrawal, mood swings, change in peer group, drastic weight loss, depression, etc. A youngster whose behavior, attitude, physical appearance, or scholastic achievement changes noticeably should be referred for assistance.[35]

> **Inhalant addiction is treated much like any other drug addiction, and various treatment options are available.**

The resource guide points out that, because the effects of an actual sniffing high come and go very quickly, it is rare to actually observe someone under the influence of an inhalant. However, parents and teachers should look for some clear signs, including disorientation, dazed appearance, chemical odor on breath, slurred speech, and coordination difficulties. If these symptoms are observed, help should be sought immediately. Parents and teachers are also being taught to remain calm if they actually catch someone in the act of sniffing. Causing an adrenaline rush in an abuser who is breathing in compressed air, for example, can kill that person.

Finally, certain products and paraphernalia are usually associated with inhalant abuse. While it can be difficult to notice inhalant abuse paraphernalia because the products being abused are everyday items, people can look for some clues. For example, parents should be aware of how empty or full their chemical products are. They should keep track of the basic level of products they have in their homes and be aware of product containers that are frequently empty without explanation. Rags, clothes, and cotton balls with chemical odors can also be a cause for concern, as are plastic bags with chemical stains or smells.

Peer Pressure

While parents and teachers are certainly a strong line of defense against inhalant abuse, educational campaigns also focus on the importance of peer pressure. In an article published in *Pediatrics and Child Health*, the Canadian Pediatrics Society points out, "Peer pressure is a powerful force contributing to initial experimentation."[36] Results from the Australian National Drug Strategy Household Survey indicate that 41 percent of the people who tried inhalants said they did so because of their friends. With this in mind, organizations like the National Inhalant Prevention Coalition work to combat this peer pressure with a different kind of peer pressure—peer pressure to avoid inhalants. It is also a part of educational campaigns to teach children the signs of inhalant abuse and tell them who to go to if they suspect their friends of huffing or sniffing.

How Is Inhalant Abuse Treated?

Treatment of inhalant abuse should be sought as early as possible. Many centers are trained in the treatment of inhalant addiction. Inhalant addiction is treated much like any other drug addiction, and various treatment options are available. In *Understanding Substance Addictions*, Sophia F. Dziegielewski explains treatment options for young inhalant abusers:

> It is generally advisable, if possible, to refer the adolescent to a short-stay treatment program so he or she can achieve abstinence from the substance with the support and structure of a treatment regimen. Family involvement in treatment is crucial, in the inpatient phase and in subsequent outpatient therapies, to help the client to maintain abstinence from the substance and to address underlying social and emotional issues.[37]

Although the best way to avoid the dangers of inhalant abuse is to never try it, even once, treatment for those who have become addicted is critical to saving their lives. With the involvement of parents, loved ones, teachers, and friends, inhalant abuse can be controlled. Survey data indicates that awareness programs most likely had a positive impact on inhalant abuse. The United States and countries all over the world will continue to struggle with inhalant abuse, however, because, though very dangerous, it is a cheap high.

How Can Inhalant Use Be Controlled?

66All we hear about is methamphetamine, but three times the number of kids use inhalants as meth. Sometimes I get jealous: I wish there was something 'sexy' about inhalants.**99**

—Harvey Weiss, "As Inhalant Group Marks Anniversary, Founder Airs Hopes, Concerns," March 16, 2007. www.jointogether.org.

Weiss is the founder and director of the National Inhalant Prevention Coalition. The NIPC is an organization devoted to educating the public about the dangers of inhalant abuse.

66[Decline in the perceived dangers of inhalants] continues to suggest the need for greater attention to this class of drugs in media messages and in-school programming.**99**

—Lloyd Johnston, "Teen Drug Use Down but Progress Halts Among Youngest Teens," University of Michigan News Service, December 19, 2005. www.monitoringthefuture.org.

Johnston is a research professor for the Survey Research Center and a distinguished senior research scientist at the Institute for Social Research at the University of Michigan. He has conducted major research studies on drug use in the United States.

* Editor's Note: While the definition of a primary source can be narrowly or broadly defined, for the purposes of Compact Research, a primary source consists of: 1) results of original research presented by an organization or researcher; 2) eyewitness accounts of events, personal experience, or work experience; 3) first-person editorials offering pundits' opinions; 4) government officials presenting political plans and/or policies; 5) representatives of organizations presenting testimony or policy.

"An individual who reaches age 21 without smoking, using drugs, or abusing alcohol is virtually certain never to do so. This means that American adolescents and their families hold the key to a drug-free America."

—Commission on Substance Abuse Among America's Adolescents, "Substance Abuse and the American Adolescent," 1997.

The Commission on Substance Abuse Among America's Adolescents is funded by the Carnegie Corporation of New York, Primerica Financial Services, and the Robert Wood Johnson Foundation to study substance abuse among youth in the United States.

"Studies show many young people try inhalation out of curiosity before getting hooked. . . . It is best not to be argumentative because it will not prevent the spread of the problem."

—Razak Lajis, "Inhalant Abuse," *PRN Bulletin* & Articles. www.prn2.usm.my.

Lajis is a pharmacist at the National Poison Centre, Universiti Sains Malaysia, Penang. He is the author of several articles offering information about and solutions for drug abuse in Malaysia.

"We added the oil of mustard to the formula nationwide. Sales dropped and we saw a decrease in the incidents and complaints from law enforcement and doctors. Oil of mustard was effective; we've used it ever since."

—Guy Carynski, quoted in Monika Bauerlein, "The Sweet Smell of Success," *Citypages*, 1993. http://pangaea.org.

Carynski is regulatory affairs director for Testor Corporation, a company that makes model-glue in Rockford, Illinois. Carynski has been a vocal advocate of reducing abuse of the company's products by adolescents.

❝Early intervention needs to be encouraged. Without intervention, inhalant abuse will not be simply outgrown.❞

—Dan Malesevich and Tom Jadin, "Of Huffers and Huffing: A Survey of Adolescent Inhalant Abuse," Treatment Improvement Exchange, 2007. www.treatment.org.

Malesevich and Jadin are social workers at the Winnebago Mental Health Institute in Winnebago, Wisconsin. Their efforts are targeted toward preventing inhalant abuse rather than attempting to cure the addiction once it is established.

....

❝The use of inhalants is a big concern. These products are legal and result in irreparable brain damage and death. Make no mistake—SAMHSA will continue to educate America on the dangers of inhalants.❞

—Charles Curie, "Advocates Urge Greater Focus on Perils of Inhalant Use," *Psychiatric News*, 2004. http://pn.psychiatryonline.org.

Curie is the director of the Substance Abuse and Mental Health Services Administration (SAMHSA). A division of the U.S. Department of Health and Human Services, SAMHSA works to improve the quality and availability of substance abuse prevention, addiction treatment, and mental health services.

....

❝If substance abuse is to be tackled, then the people who should lead this effort must be youth themselves, since they know their own needs better than anyone else.❞

—Selim Iltus and Kim Sabo, in UNODC and Global Youth Network, *A Participatory Handbook for Youth Drug Prevention Programmes: A Guide for Development and Improvement*. New York: United Nations, 2002. www.unodc.org.

Iltus is codirector of the Children's Environments Research Group, City University of New York. Sabo works with the group as a participatory planning and evaluation consultant.

....

66Adults can help young people stay away from inhalants by helping them set goals for themselves, build their self confidence and teach them to stand up against peer pressure.99

—Anne Gadomski. "October's Child Health Month Focuses on Preventing Inhalant Abuse," Basset Health Care.
www.bassett.org.

Gadomski is a pediatrician with the Bassett Research Institute in Cooperstown, New York. She works to emphasize the importance of substance abuse prevention and life-skills development for all youth.

66During the past 18 months, I've spoken with over 4500 New Mexico youth. They know everything about inhalants except they're poison and harmful.99

—Trish Hatch, "Secrets of the Streets: Things Our Youth Are Doing That You Need to Know About," New Mexico
School Counselor Association, 2007.

Trish Hatch is director of the school counseling graduate program at San Diego State University. She provides training for counselors in dealing with critical student issues, such as inhalant abuse.

66It's not illegal—that's what makes this so difficult. Kids don't see a spray-paint can bust; you can't arrest a kid for buying spray paint.99

—Janine Kravetz, Huffing Despite Deaths of Two Teens Last Year, Inhalant Abuse Among Youths Rises in Bay County,
Michigan," 2005. www.drug-rehabs.org.

Kravetz is the prevention coordinator for Bay Area Social Intervention Services of Bay County, Michigan.

66When I do glue, it makes my imagination so good. I have no anxiety or pain. I imagine myself in a big comfortable house. I have money and all the kids around me have plates of food, warm tea and new clothes.99

—Amad Adel, quoted in Emily Wax, "Young and Homeless Fill Africa's City Streets," *Washington Post*, 2005. www.familycare.org.

Amad is a 13-year-old homeless boy living in Sudan in Africa. Wax, a reporter for the *Washington Post*, quotes Amad's response to a counselor who offered him room in a shelter on condition that he stop sniffing glue.

How Can Inhalant Use Be Controlled?

- **CleanSafe** is an alternative brand of compressed air. Its manufacturers have added bitterant or bittergent technology. This **"bitter agent"** is highly irritating to nasal passages and designed to stop abusers from "dusting." Another compressed air manufacturer, Falcon, is also adding deterrents to its products.

- According to the research of members of the University of Wisconsin Law School, **10 states** have included inhalants specifically in their laws against driving under the influence of intoxicants.

- Research shows that when **adolescents know the facts** about drugs, such as inhalants, they are more likely to avoid them and make healthy choices about their future.

- A major problem with addressing the **dangers** of inhalants is that many young people may admit they have sniffed a few toxic items, but they often deny that that is abuse.

- Some counselors argue that the most effective way to prevent children from **engaging in inhalant abuse** is to point out that it is most often done by sixth through ninth graders, making the practice "kid stuff." Stressing that point, rather than pointing to dangers, may have the best results.

- While the Internet can provide a **wealth of knowledge** about the dangers of drugs and how to prevent drug use, a 2005 study found that the Internet leads adolescent drug users to try new drugs and drug combinations, take steps to minimize the harmful effects of drugs, and modify the use of preferred drugs.

State Inhalant Legislation

According to the National Inhalant Prevention Coalition, many states have passed laws in an attempt to curb inhalant abuse. Some states have passed legislation limiting minors' access to certain chemicals, and others have laws against the inhalation of chemicals for intoxication. No federal laws exist, and state laws are difficult to enforce.

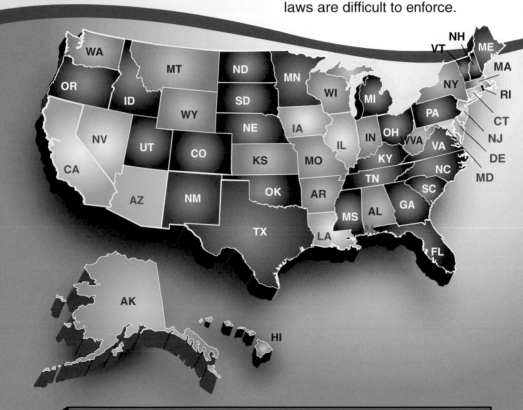

Sale of certain chemical compounds illegal in some way

Illegal to inhale chemicals for intoxication

Laws against both sale and inhaling for intoxication

Retailers to maintain registry of sales and illegal to inhale for intoxication

Retailers to maintain registry of sales and inhalants required to have noxious deterrents

No Legislation

Source: National Inhalant Prevention Coalition, "State Inhalant Legislation," 2007. www.inhalants.org.

Common Terms Associated with Inhalants

Organizations devoted to educating the public about inhalant abuse stress the importance of knowledge of the slang associated with a drug. Parents, especially, are encouraged to be aware of common street terms associated with inhalant abuse.

Slang Term	Definition
Air Blast	Inhalants
Bagging	Using inhalants
Buzz Bomb	Nitrous Oxide
Climax	Isobutyl Nitrate
Glading	Using inhalants
Gluey	Sniffing or inhaling glue
Huffer	Inhalants abuser
Poor Man's Pot	Inhalants

Source: Office of National Drug Control Policy, "Drug Facts: Inhalants," 2007. www.whitehousedrugpolicy.gov.

- No federal system exists in the United States for **tracking deaths** related to inhalants. One Virginia study, however, examined 39 inhalant fatalities and found that the average age of victims was **19**.

- Recognizing the **toxic and criminal effects** of inhalants, some police departments will not hire candidates who have used inhalants within 10 years before applying.

- When attempts have been made to put **warning labels** on abusable inhalant products, this may actually have had the opposite of the desired effect. Children were simply more aware of which products were sniffable.

- According to a 2001 Australian National Drug Strategy Household Survey, people who had abused inhalants listed **"curiosity"** as the most common reason they started using inhalants. The second most common reason was **"friends."**

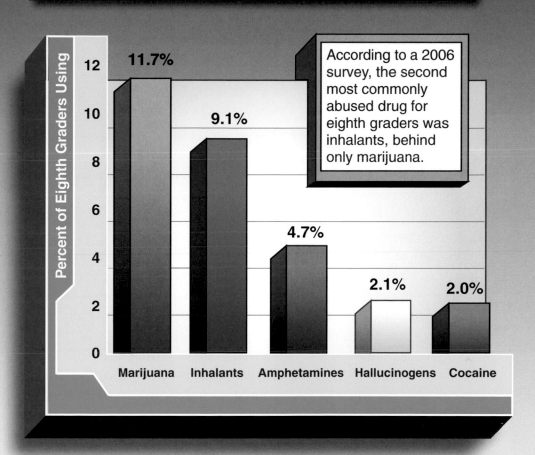

2006 Drug Use Prevalence for Eighth Graders

Percent of Eighth Graders Using

- Marijuana: 11.7%
- Inhalants: 9.1%
- Amphetamines: 4.7%
- Hallucinogens: 2.1%
- Cocaine: 2.0%

According to a 2006 survey, the second most commonly abused drug for eighth graders was inhalants, behind only marijuana.

Source: Monitoring the Future Study, University of Michigan, 2006.

Key People and Advocacy Groups

Community Anti-Drug Coalitions of America (CADCA): CADCA was founded in 1992 and is an organization of over 5000 community coalitions that work together to organize and develop programs to coordinate anti-drug efforts. CADCA creates a comprehensive, community-based approach to drug prevention and education.

D.A.R.E. (Drug Abuse Resistance Education): D.A.R.E. was founded in 1983 by Los Angeles Police chief Daryl Gates. It is a non-profit organization that has become an international leader in educating youth about drugs, gangs, and violence. D.A.R.E. offers programs to the public schools for all grade levels. These programs are taught by local law enforcement agents. According to its Web site, D.A.R.E. programs exist in 80 percent of the school districts in the United States and in 54 countries around the world.

Kim and Marissa Manlove: The Manloves lost their 15-year-old son to inhalant abuse in 2001. They now share their son's story to help both parents and children understand the dangers of inhalants. They speak at schools and maintain Web pages serving as both memorial for their son and education for the public.

National Inhalant Prevention Coalition (NIPC): The NIPC is devoted to education about the prevention of inhalant abuse, particularly among young children and teens. The coalition offers information about the dangers of inhalants and signs of abuse, as well as important links related to inhalants for both parents and children.

National Institute on Drug Abuse (NIDA): NIDA leads the nation in bringing the power of science to bear on drug abuse and addiction. NIDA supports and conducts research across a broad range of disciplines and ensures the rapid and effective dissemination and use of the results of that research to significantly improve prevention, treatment, and policy as it relates to drug abuse and addiction.

New England Inhalant Abuse Prevention Coalition: Since the 1990s the New England Inhalant Abuse Prevention Coalition has worked to reduce inhalant abuse by creating statewide inhalant task forces or teams. The mission of these teams and task forces is to help their states' prevention systems be more effective in addressing inhalant abuse.

The Partnership for a Drug-Free America: The Partnership for a Drug-Free America is a nonprofit coalition of communication, health, medical, and educational professionals who work to reduce illicit drug use. Its research-based, educational campaigns are spread through all forms of media, including TV, radio, print advertisements, and the Internet.

Nora Volkow: Nora Volkow is a physician and became director of the National Institute on Drug Abuse (NIDA) in May 2003. She is an international leader in drug addiction research and brain imaging. Before becoming director of NIDA, Volkow was a professor in the department of psychiatry and associate dean of the medical school at the State University of New York–Stony Brook. She has a long record of accomplishment in drug addiction research and is a recognized expert on the brain's dopamine system. Her research focuses on the brains of addicted, obese, and aging individuals.

Harvey Weiss: Weiss is the founder and director of the National Inhalant Prevention Coalition in Austin, Texas. This organization works to educate the public about the dangers of inhalants, and Weiss has helped launch a massive media campaign against inhalants.

Jeff Williams: Jeff Williams is a police officer in the Cleveland, Ohio, area who lost his son to inhalant abuse in 2005. Williams has since worked to spread the word to parents about the dangers of inhalant abuse. He is cited by the makers of the compressed air "Dust-Off" on their educational Web page referring the public to their new formula that includes a deterrent.

Chronology

1275
Ether is discovered by Spanish chemist Raymundus Lullus.

1831–1832
Chloroform is discovered at about the same time and independently by three scientists: Samuel Guthrie, Justus von Liebig, and Eugene Soubeiran.

1776
Humphry Davy synthesizes nitrous oxide.

1840
Dentist Horace Wells witnesses the benefits of nitrous oxide to alleviate pain at a stage show.

1275   1775   1830 1840 1850   1920   1940

1772
Nitrous oxide is discovered by English scientist Joseph Priestley.

1847
Dr. James Simpson introduces to Scotland chloroform as an anesthesia during childbirth. Simpson was later knighted by Queen Victoria for this work.

1799
Humphry Davy proposes using nitrous oxide to alleviate pain during surgeries, but no on tests this possibility.

1920s
Ether is a popular recreational drug in the United States during the prohibition of alcohol.

1940s
First outbreak of gasoline sniffing reported in media in Pennsylvania.

1960
FDA eliminates the need for a prescription for alkyl nitrite, making it available over the counter.

2005
U.S. Consumer Product Safety Commission identifies more than 1,000 different products being misused as inhalants.

1961
Glue sniffing epidemic begins in Denver, Colorado.

1990s
During the 1990s inhalant abuse among adolescents reaches an all-time high.

1969
FDA reinstates prescription status of alkyl nitrite.

1960   1970   1980   1990   2000   2005

1968
Thirteen states have passed legislation against glue sniffing.

1992
The National Inhalant Prevention Coalition is founded.

2000
The World Health Organization reports that inhalant abuse is a problem among tens of millions of children and adolescents from all over the world.

1962
The first known law against glue sniffing is passed in Anaheim, California.

1959
Earliest reported cases of glue sniffing in Colorado and Arizona are cited in medical literature.

2003
The United Kingdom reports 2,103 inhalant deaths since 1971.

Glossary

bagging: Slant term for using inhalants by inhaling them from a bag, often a sandwich or grocery bag.

bitterant or bittergent: A chemical added to a product to give it a bad smell and make the product difficult to inhale.

chroming: The slang term for inhaling aerosol paints.

deterrent: Another name for a bitterant or bittergent; a chemical added to a product to deter inhaling.

Glading: Slang term for using inhalants, referencing the air freshener that can be abused as an inhalant.

gluey: The slang term for inhaling glue for intoxication.

huffing: Slang term for using a bag to inhale a chemical for intoxication.

inhalant abuse: Intentionally inhaling a substance that gives off a vapor or gas for its intoxicating effects.

Medusa: Slant term for inhalants

nanging: The slang term for inhaling nitrous oxide from whipped cream cans.

Sudden Sniffing Death Syndrome: A syndrome that results in death when an inhalant abuser is surprised and adrenaline to the heart causes cardiac failure.

tolly: Slang term for toluene, a chemical contained in many inhalants.

Related Organizations

American School Health Association

7263 State Rt. 43

PO Box 708

Kent, Ohio 44240

phone: (330) 678-1601

e-mail: asha@ashaweb.org • Web site: www.ashaweb.org

The American School Health Association is an organization of school professionals who work together to protect the health of school-aged children. Founded in 1927, this organization works on a variety of issues including immunization, sexually transmitted diseases, and drug awareness.

Do It Now Foundation

PO Box 27568

Tempe, AZ 85285

phone: (480) 736-0771

e-mail: email@doitnow • Web site: www.doitnow.org

The Do It Now Foundation calls itself "America's Drug Education Connection." This organization develops educational pamphlets on a wide variety of drugs and some other topics. Do It Now has also developed public service announcements.

Drug Abuse Resistance Education (D.A.R.E.)

PO Box 512090

Los Angeles, CA 90051

phone: (800) 223-DARE or (800) 215-0575

Web site: www.dare.com

D.A.R.E.'s primary mission is to provide children with the information and skills they need to live drug-and-violence-free lives. It also works to establish positive relationships between students and law enforcement, teachers, parents, and other community leaders. It was founded it 1983 and developed curricula to be used in K-12 classrooms.

Drug Enforcement Administration (DEA)

2401 Jefferson Davis Hwy., Suite 300

Alexandria, VA 22301

phone: (800) 882-9539

Web site: www.dea.gov

The Drug Enforcement Administration works to enforce the controlled substances laws and regulations in the United States. The DEA coordinates with federal, state, and local law enforcement agencies on mutual drug enforcement efforts. It also recommends and supports programs aimed at reducing the availability and use of illicit drugs.

Drug Free America Foundation, Inc.

2600 9th St. N., Suite 200

St. Petersburg, FL 33704

phone: (727) 828-0212

Web site: www.dfaf.org

Drug Free America Foundation, Inc. is a drug prevention and policy organization committed to developing, promoting, and sustaining global strategies, policies, and laws that will reduce illegal drug use, drug addiction, drug-related injury, and death.

National Drug Intelligence Center (NDIC)

Office of Policy and Interagency Affairs, U.S. Department of Justice

Robert F. Kennedy Bldg., Rm. 1335

950 Pennsylvania Ave. NW

Washington, DC 20530

phone: (202) 532-4040

Web site: www.usdoj.gov

Established in 1993, the National Drug Intelligence Center (NDIC) is a component of the U.S. Department of Justice and a member of the intelligence community. The General Counterdrug Intelligence Plan, signed by the president in February 2000, designated NDIC as the nation's principal center for strategic domestic counterdrug intelligence. Its mission is to support national policy makers and law enforcement decision makers with strategic domestic drug intelligence, to support intelligence community counterdrug efforts, and to produce national, regional, and state drug threat assessments.

National Inhalant Prevention Coalition

322-A Thompson St.

Chattanooga, TN 37405

phone: (800) 269-4237

e-mail: nipc@io.com • Web site: www.inhalants.org

The National Inhalant Prevention Coalition is devoted to education about the prevention of inhalant abuse, particularly among young children and teens. This organization developed the National Inhalants and Poisons Awareness Week, an annual media event in March devoted to inhalant education. The NIPC Web site offers information about the dangers of inhalants, signs of abuse, as well as important links related to inhalants for both parents and children.

National Institute on Drug Abuse (NIDA)

6001 Executive Blvd., Rm. 5213

Bethesda, MD 20892-9561

phone: (301) 443-1124

e-mail: information@nida.nih.gov • Web site: www.nida.nih.gov

The National Institute on Drug Abuse's mission is to lead the nation in bringing the power of science to bear on drug abuse and addiction. NIDA was established in 1974, and in October 1992 it became part of the National Institutes of Health, Department of Health and Human Services. The institute is organized into divisions and offices, each of which plays an important role in programs of drug abuse research.

Office of National Drug Control Policy

Drug Policy Information Clearinghouse

PO Box 6000

Rockville, MD 20849-6000

phone: (800) 666-3332 • fax: (301) 519-5212

Web site: www.whitehousedrugpolicy.gov

The White House Office of National Drug Control Policy (ONDCP), a component of the Executive Office of the President, was established by the Anti-Drug Abuse Act of 1988. The principal purpose of ONDCP is to establish policies, priorities, and objectives for the nation's drug control program. The goals of the program are to reduce illicit drug use, manufacturing, and trafficking, drug-related crime and violence, and drug-related health consequences. To achieve these goals, the director of ONDCP is charged with producing the National Drug Control Strategy.

For Further Research

Books

Sophia F. Dziegielewski, *Understanding Substance Addictions: Assessment and Intervention*. Chicago: Lyceum, 2005.

Glen R. Hanson, Peter J. Venturelli, and Annette E. Fleckenstein, *Drugs and Society*. Boston: Jones and Bartlett, 2006.

Icon Health, *The Official Patient's Sourcebook on Inhalants Dependence*. San Diego: Icon Health, 2002.

Johnson Institute, *What to Teach Kids About Inhalants*. Center City, MN: Hazelden, 1998.

Robert M. Julien, *A Primer of Drug Action*. 10th ed. New York: Worth, 2005.

Cynthia Kuhn, Scott Swartzwelder, and Wilkie Wilson, *Buzzed: The Straight Facts About the Most Used and Abused Drugs from Alcohol to Ecstasy*. New York: Norton, 1998.

Sandra Lawton, *Drug Information for Teens*. Detroit: Omnigraphics, 2006.

William A. McKim, *Drugs and Behavior*. 5th ed. Upper Saddle River, NJ: Prentice Hall, 2003.

Darious A. Rastegar and Michael I. Fingerhood, *Addiction Medicine: An Evidence-Based Handbook*. Philadelphia: Lippincott, Williams, and Wilkins, 2005.

Andrew Weil and Winifred Rosen, *From Chocolate to Morphine: Everything You Need to Know About Mind-Altering Drugs*. Rev. ed. Boston: Houghton Mifflin, 1998.

Periodicals

Melissa Abramovitz, "The Dangers of Inhalants," *Current Health*, October 2003.

Alcoholism and Drug Abuse Weekly, "Teen Use of Inhalants Rising," March 2007.

Canadian Pediatrics Society, "Inhalant Abuse," *Pediatrics and Child Health*, 1998.

Ron Chepesiuk, "Resurgence of Teen Inhalant Use," *Environmental Health Perspectives*, December 2005.

Gregory F. Fritz, "Inhalant Abuse Among Children and Adolescents: More Common and More Dangerous than We Think," *Brown University Child and Adolescent Behavior Letter*, December 2003.

Marianne D. Hurst, "Inhalant Use," *Education Week*, June 2004.

Teddi Dineley Johnson, "New Study Shows 1.8 Million Youth Use Inhalants," *Nation's Health*, May 2006.

Donna Leinwand, "Girls Are Now 'Huffing' More than Boys, Abuse Study Says," *USA Today* (magazine), March 2007.

Michael T. Lynskey, "Screening for Inhalant Abuse in Children and Adolescents," *American Family Physician*, September 2003.

Julie Metha, "Whiff of Trouble," *Current Health*, September 2006.

Judy Monroe, "Inhalants Smell like Trouble," *Current Health*, April/May 2004.

Bryan O'Dell, "Everything Under the Kitchen Sink," *Family Safety and Health*, Summer 2006.

Christopher Ringwalt, Susan T. Ennett, and Kathleen D. Holt, "An Outcome Evaluation of Project DARE (Drug Abuse Resistance Education)," *Health Education Research*, 1991.

Christina A. Samuels, "Teen Inhalant Abuse Seen Rising Slightly," *Education Week*, April 2006.

Science Teacher, "The Facts About Inhalants," April/May 2006.

Jessica L. Tonn, "Good and Bad News on Teenage Drug Use," *Education Week*, January 2005.

———, "Illegal Drug Use," *Education Week*, January 2006.

Libby Tucker, "Fatal Choice," *Choices*, January 2007.

Li-Tzy Wu, Daniel J. Pilowsky, and William E. Schlenger, "High Prevalence of Substance Use Disorders Among Adolescents Who Use Marijuana and Inhalants," *Drug and Alcohol Dependence*, April 2005.

Li-Tzy Wu and Christopher Ringwalt, "Inhalant Use and Disorders Among Adults in the United States," *Drug and Alcohol Dependence*, October 2006.

Internet Sources

American Council for Drug Education, "Basic Facts About Drugs: Inhalants," 1999. www.acde.org/common/Inhalant.

Drug Free America Foundation, "Inhalants," 2007. www.dfaf.org.

Jennifer James, "Inhalants: Why to Pass on Gas," Do It Now Foundation, June 2002. www.doitnow.org.

National Institute on Drug Abuse, "Mind over Matter: Inhalants," *NIDA for Teens*, January 2007. http://teens.drugabuse.gov/mom/mom_inha1.asp.

National Youth Anti-Drug Media Campaign, "Inhalants." www.theanti drug.com.

Source Notes

Overview

1. Sophia F. Dziegielewski, *Understanding Substance Addictions: Assessment and Intervention.* Chicago: Lyceum, 2005. pp. 228–29.
2. Falcon, "New Dust-Off Formula Deters Inhalant Abuse," October 2006. www.falconsafety.com.
3. Carol Moore, "The Cheapest High," Connect for Kids, April 25, 2005. www.connectforkids.org.
4. Drugstory.org, "Huffing: An Interview with Harvey Weiss." www.drugstory.org.
5. National Inhalant Prevention Coalition, "Inhalants," March 2007. www.inhalants.org.
6. Office of National Drug Control Policy, "Drug Facts: Inhalants," March 2007. www.whitehousedrugpolicy.org.

What Are Inhalants?

7. William A. McKim, *Drugs and Behavior*, 5th ed., Upper Saddle River, NJ: Prentice Hall, 2003. p. 160.
8. Robert M. Julien, *A Primer of Drug Addiction*, 10th ed., New York: Worth, 2005. p. 159.
9. Jennifer James, *All About Inhalants: A Special Report for Young People*, Do It Now Foundation, 2007. www.doitnow.org/pages/143.html.

What Are the Risks of Inhalant Abuse?

10. Cynthia Kuhn, Scott Swartzwelder, and Wilkie Wilson, *Buzzed: The Straight Facts About the Most Used and Abused Drugs from Alcohol to Ecstasy.* New York: Norton, 1998. p. 114.
11. Quoted in Barbara Mikkelson, "Dusted Off," July 2005. www.snopes.com.
12. Quoted in CBC News, "Parents Warned of 'Dusting' Solvent Abuse," June 2005. www.cbc.ca.
13. Quoted in Serenity Lane, "Inhalant Abuse," 2005. www.serenitylane.org.
14. Recovery Connection, "Inhalants," 2006. www.recoveryconnection.org.
15. U.S. Drug Enforcement Administration, "Inhalants," August 2006. www.dea.gov.
16. National Inhalant Prevention Coalition, "Inhalants," March 2007. www.inhalants.org.
17. U.S. Drug Enforcement Administration, "Inhalants."
18. Hazelden Foundation, "Awareness of Inhalant Abuse Needs to Start Early," March 2006. www.hazelden.org.
19. U.S. Drug Enforcement Administration, "What's Up with Inhalants?" www.dea.gov.

How Does Inhalant Abuse Affect Society?

20. Glen R. Hanson, Peter J. Venturelli, and Annette E. Fleckenstein, *Drugs and Society.* Boston: Jones and Bartlett, 2006. p. 425.
21. U.S. Drug Enforcement Administration, "Inhalants."
22. National Inhalant Prevention Coalition, "Inhalants."
23. Dziegielewski, *Understanding Substance Addictions.*
24. Australian Drug Foundation, "Drug Info Clearinghouse: Drug Laws," 2007. http://druginfo.adf.org.au.
25. National Inhalant Prevention Coalition, "Inhalants."
26. National Inhalant Prevention Coalition, "Inhalants."
27. Christopher J. Mumola and Jennifer C.

Karberg, "Drug Use and Dependence, State and Federal Prisons, 2004," U.S. Department of Justice, October 2006. www.ojp.usdoj.gov.

28. National Inhalant Prevention Coalition, "Inhalants."

29. National Inhalant Prevention Coalition, "Inhalants."

30. National Inhalant Prevention Coalition, "Inhalants."

How Can Inhalant Use Be Controlled?

31. Christopher Ringwalt, Susan T. Ennett, and Kathleen D. Holt, "An Outcome Evaluation of Project DARE (Drug Abuse Resistance Education)," *Health Education Research*, 1991. p. 327.

32. Quoted in Drug Abuse Resistance Education, "Illinois DARE Assessment," 2001. www.dare.com.

33. Quoted in Partnership for a Drug Free America, "New Generation of Teens Abusing Inhalants," April 2006. www.drugfree.org.

34. Quoted in Partnership for a Drug Free America, "New Generation of Teens Abusing Inhalants."

35. Isabel Burk, "Inhalant Prevention Resource Guide," Virginia Department of Education, 2001.

36. Canadian Pediatrics Society, "Inhalant Abuse," *Pediatrics and Child Health*, 1998. p. 123.

37. Dziegielewski, *Understanding Substance Addictions*. p. 233.

List of Illustrations

Index

About the Author

Crystal McCage holds a PhD in rhetoric from Texas Woman's University. She lives in Bend, Oregon, with her husband, Wesley, and their son Joseph. This is her second book for ReferencePoint Press.